SO MUCH FROM SO LITTLE

THE STORY OF AN ORDINARY GUY WHO DID EXTRAORDINARY THINGS

GRAHAM M. DACRE CBE

River Publishing & Media Ltd
Bradbourne Stables
East Malling
Kent
ME19 6DZ
United Kingdom

info@river-publishing.co.uk

Special thanks to Nigel Pickover and the Eastern Daily Press for the use of a number of images in the picture section.

ISBN 978-1-908393-57-9
Cover design by www.spiffingcovers.com
Printed in the United Kingdom

CONTENTS

WHAT OTHERS ARE SAYING...

Underneath Graham Dacre's self-effacing, often humorous, and always easy-going style, lies a tenacious and focused entrepreneur who has enjoyed great success. His story is an absorbing and fascinating read, which speaks about the highs and lows of entrepreneurship without pulling any punches. But what shines through these pages is the centrality and importance of Graham's faith in all he does, and his commitment to live for something bigger than himself.
The Baroness Cox, Founder and President of Humanitarian Aid Relief Trust (HART)

I have been privileged to know Graham as a friend for many years and am delighted to see his story in print. Many autobiographies of people who have been successful in business are little more than exercises in self-glorification, and should be read with caution. This is refreshingly different. For a start it's genuinely *helpful*; it's full of invaluable and hard-earned lessons about how to succeed in business without losing your soul. It's also tremendously *honest*; for example, Graham's account of how he was tricked out of more money than most of us can ever conceive of is a painful but invaluable tale well worth learning from. Above all it is a *humble* book; Graham loses no opportunity to testify to the fact that God helped him in both the good and bad times. Graham is very grateful to God for His grace; I am in turn grateful to Graham for this book.
Revd Canon J.John

Graham Dacre's story is full of significant life lessons but, most of all, it reminds us that God invites us to participate with Him in fulfilling His purposes, not as passive spectators but as active participants. Graham's honesty, courage and even mistakes demonstrate that the secret to life is found in trusting God and in seeking His purposes above all else. This is a compelling and entertaining read but, like the book of Proverbs, it carries many nuggets of wisdom worth savouring.
Jonathan Lamb, CEO and minister-at-large, Keswick Ministries

There doesn't seem much comfort for the wealthy in the teaching of Jesus. In the Sermon on the Mount it is the poor, the meek and the heartbroken who are blessed. Those who find faith in Christ as well as financial success in business are sometimes looked upon with suspicion, even by their fellow Christians.

Graham Dacre is well aware of this. This illuminating book describes his struggles and mistakes as well as his successes. It is also clear what has brought him the deepest joy in his life – his family and his encounter with the living God.

This is more than a story of business deals, though they are fascinating. It's about blessings received. I know from my own experience that quite a lot of what Graham has done so generously and constructively for the people of Norwich and Norfolk gets little coverage here. I'm sure that's because Graham is seeking to emulate St Paul who, when he was tempted to boast (and he had plenty to boast about), did so only to give glory to the God and Father of the Lord Jesus Christ. I pray that this book will be a blessing to many.
Rt Revd Graham James, Lord Bishop of Norwich

Graham Dacre has had a most interesting life with remarkable achievements, guided by his faith. This valuable book shares many of the lessons he has learned in an accessible way.
Richard Jewson, Lord Lieutenant of Norfolk

Reading the confessions of a man who I have known for over 25 years was a revelation. Ever the entrepreneur Graham Dacre has given us two books for the price of one. The written story and the story written between the lines. You can read his book in a few hours and learn lessons that will last a life time and beyond. No doubt Graham has climbed the precarious golden ladder of success but you the reader must discern if it's leaning against the right wall.
John Drake, CEO YMCA Norfolk 1979/2009; Sheriff of Norwich 2006

This book, drawn from the journey of someone who has always prioritised a passion for his faith over every other consideration, is written with both transparency and vulnerability. Too often those who epitomise success in their personal sphere gloss over the

challenges and disappointments that go with the territory, and may even be essential to a trajectory towards the pinnacle that has been reached. This book honours the part that God has played as well as the leadership and financial acumen of its author.
John Glass, General Superintendent Elim Churches

I've known Graham for several years and the one thing that has always impressed me about him is that, even though he has considerable wealth, it hasn't changed his character one bit. Just as it was at the beginning of his career – when he had little money to speak of – his faith has remained central to who he is and what he does. He still has a heart for God and a desire to help build the local church. He is a great example of how to be a successful, kingdom-minded entrepreneur. For anyone who has a similar desire to make an impact on their world, this is required reading.
Stephen Derbyshire, Senior Pastor, City Gates Church, Ilford

Seldom have I had an opportunity to read an autobiography written with such honesty, openness and transparency. Graham shares his life story and his amazing success in the auto industry in simple, everyday language, mixed with humour and entertaining narrative, as he gives account of some of his many experiences. He does not shy away from the mistakes made along the way. He gives all credit to our Almighty God for His blessing and favour, whilst providing practical, tried, tested and proven steps for young entrepreneurs, as well as some excellent character building advice. Graham gives the reader more than a mere glimpse into the heart, mind and soul of a man committed to living life for something other than success in business, wealth and personal gain. His is a life worth living for a far greater purpose. I firmly believe that he is succeeding right now in achieving all that he was born to do. Our friendship has been a blessing to me and I am truly honoured to call Graham, his wife Julie and family, my lifelong friends!
Kyffin Simpson, K.A., C.B.E., Hon. L.L.D., UWI

I'd like to agree with this book's strapline, "the story of an ordinary guy who did extraordinary things". However, there's nothing ordinary about Graham Dacre! Sure, like many of us, he comes from

humble roots, but that background has served him well. Intelligent, visionary, hard-working, tenacious, generous – and a great deal of fun to be around, as I know well. With great honesty, failure as well as success is catalogued, along with stories to make you laugh out loud. Here is brilliant counsel and advice for every would-be business entrepreneur, and anyone trying to navigate this sea called life. Enjoy this great story of a great guy, and behind it all, aided by a loving family, be prepared to meet a great and gracious God who still calls prodigals to follow Him.
Dr Steve Brady, Principal, Moorlands College, Christchurch, UK

The first time I came across Graham Dacre it was as a rather irritating noise disturbing the peace of a summers day in Norfolk. I was in my garden, Graham was in his helicopter skimming down the Wensum Valley, an almost literal case, as I later found out, of *deus ex machina*! We are close neighbours, a few miles apart, and our lives have touched each other progressively over the years: the irritating noise became a friend.

All human beings are unique. Graham's uniqueness stems from a combination of relentless energy, unwavering purpose and an almost pathological determination to change things. All men dream, usually idly and pointlessly. Graham lives to turn his dreams into reality. He has created businesses, he has built a property empire, he has established churches, he has founded and supported schools. From very little he has made a life of significance and meaning. And there is more to do! Graham has written a book, but there are many chapters still to come.
Lord David Prior of Brampton

The stories and principles contained in this book have been woven into the fabric of my life. Whilst Dad can be misunderstood, he's the real deal. He's generous and passionate about sharing the good news of Christ to everyone he meets.
Russ Dacre, MBE

"What shall we say to these things?" Those that knew my grandfather, Sedley Pimlott, will fondly recall him quoting that Bible verse from the book of Romans. More often than not he didn't say anything

further afterwards, leaving the thought hanging in mid air and the listener to fill in the rest. The passage goes on to say, *"If God be for us, who can be against us?"* This amazing story of my father's life just shows the power of having a great God walking ahead of us, making a way, where seemly impossible situations miraculously resolve themselves; of what God can achieve through one man who has a little faith in Him. I am often in awe at the deals my father has done and having read Dad's story again, I am once again awestruck. Even though I have been old enough to be aware of most of the stories in this book, it made for a fascinating read, refreshing long forgotten moments, filling in one or two extra details I was unaware of at the time – and a few stories were new to me too. Above all though, I would like to thank my father for articulating how good God has been to him and to us as a family, and for instilling in me, arguably the most basic principle in life – *Have faith in God* – for with it mountains are moved! I love you Dad.
Samuel Dacre

This is not a piece of vanity publishing from a member of the "God Squad" preaching to the choir. In this short book, Graham shares some life lessons that he hopes will benefit all who take the trouble to read it, whether they are a Christian or not. It's illuminating, frank and gives an insight into what makes the man tick, with a motivation that goes beyond the present day "me" culture. If you are curious about his "rags to riches" success, then his trials, tribulations, risk taking and belief are laid bare.
Peter Franzen OBE

I am delighted to congratulate Graham on the publication of this fascinating book. Graham's story makes compelling reading and is a marvellous example of a "can-do" attitude which can lead to great success. On top of my pleasure in supporting this publication it has been my extra joy to get to know Graham, such a force for good in our East Anglian Community. All best wishes for your continuing success.
Nigel Pickover
Editor-in-Chief
Eastern Daily Press & Norwich Evening News

DEDICATION

For Julie – the one person without whom nothing would have been possible. I cannot overstate my gratitude for your wise words and quiet, but unstinting, support over the last forty years.
You are truly amazing.
Thank you.

INTRODUCTION

What a life. What a journey. What a great adventure – and there is still more to come! Looking back, I am amazed at the things I've done. Things I never expected to do. Places I've visited that I never imagined I'd get to see. Dreams I had that ended up being wildly surpassed, and in different ways than I'd ever thought possible.

When I was 45 I told my boys that if anything happened to me whilst flying my helicopter, not to be upset – at least not for me. Even then I felt I'd experienced more than most people would in a lifetime. But thereafter I was to go on the most exciting ride of my life – the one I'm still presently experiencing – my ultimate dream of building a church that would bring glory to God and touch the lives of many people.

Recalling the events of the last 50 years has proven easier than I anticipated when I began. Memories are often like that. All we need is something to provoke us and they come flooding back. I have been surprised by just how much I did remember, once I began putting pen to paper. What was even more surprising was how the emotions attached to those memories were rekindled by the process – the joys, the satisfaction, the losses, the heartaches, the errors and the sense of failure that accompanied them at the time.

Life has its ups and downs. Looking back, there are things that we can see we got right. Then we also have regrets. With the benefit of hindsight we can usually see where we went wrong and what we would do differently, given the opportunity. But I am grateful for the fact that, overall, writing this book has filled me with a deep sense of thankfulness. I have a great gratitude towards God and a heartfelt sense of thankfulness to many others who have shared life with me.

When I finally decided to write this book, I wanted it to be much more than simply a chronological retelling of my life from my perspective. I was keen for it to serve a bigger purpose. Looking back, I can see that at every stage of my journey there were lessons to learn. At the time, some of these "life lessons" hit me with great clarity. I learned what I needed to learn, adjusted my thinking and moved on. Other lessons have presented themselves in the recollection – such as the impact of many different mentors, each of whom exerted a benignly powerful influence on me at various times. Since I have been successful in business, and since I'm frequently asked how and why that transpired, I have sought to recall episodes from my life that illustrate particular principles I've learned that will be of help to others (though this is not strictly a "business book"). It does, however, contain principles that, if observed, will vastly improve the chances of you positioning yourself for success. I hope these prove to be valuable assets for the reader in the future.

To date, my life has not been without its controversies. This book contains my take on one or two tales that have been widely publicised in the media. Some may be worried by that statement. They need not be. As someone once said, "We don't increase the brightness of our lamp by extinguishing the light of others." To those who, over the years, feel that I have upset or wronged them in any way, I apologise. To those who may feel the need to say sorry to me, there is no need. Along life's journey there are only a few who I don't remember with anything other than great affection. I am grateful to all those who have added to the colour and richness of life's tapestry!

Finally, I have endeavoured to be as straightforward and transparent as possible in recounting the episodes herein. I realise that doing so renders me vulnerable to further criticism. In the event, I am not worried. After all these years I would miss it if it weren't there! I hope you enjoy reading about the journey as much as I've enjoyed living it. I am still amazed that so much could have been achieved from so little.

Graham M. Dacre CBE

PART 1
AN UNEXPECTED ADVENTURE

1
LIVING FOR SOMETHING GREATER THAN OURSELVES

"A hero is someone who has given his or her life to something bigger than oneself."

– JOSEPH CAMPBELL

"I don't know what my calling is, but I want to be here for a bigger reason. I strive to be like the greatest people who have ever lived."

– WILL SMITH

Getting started in business and making your mark on the world can be exciting, adrenaline-fuelled stuff. Entrepreneurs get a buzz of satisfaction from clinching a new deal, breaking into a new market, launching a new initiative. It's only natural. It's what they were born to do.

I have not been a typical entrepreneur in that my faith in God takes precedence over the need to grow a business and make money. Yes, I was driven to succeed. Yes, I wanted to make money. But early on God got my attention and helped me to see something vital. Whilst being successful was, in and of itself, a laudable goal, He had much bigger plans in mind. I needed to grasp the fact that I was living for a purpose bigger than myself.

Herein lies one of the greatest revelations I've learned over the years. We are more joyful, more peaceful and more prosperous when we are living for something greater than "me". If the only purpose of generating enormous wealth is enormous self-indulgence, where is the meaning in that? But in living beyond ourselves, we truly live. Here is something of my journey into learning this truth.

BEGINNINGS

In 1972 there was a garage in Long Stratton that was to be sold by auction. The premises included a showroom, a workshop, petrol pumps, a used car sales forecourt and even a relatively new bungalow. When the bidding ended and the hammer fell my grandad, Archie Friday, had bought it on behalf of my parents for £12,000. To begin trading Grandad arranged loans amounting to £10,000 and created an advert in the local press for the rebranded "Long Stratton Autos", that included the invitation to "Mr Friday's Weekly Car Chat". It went down well with the locals and the business began to get going.

At the time I was working at Boulton and Paul on Riverside Road as a computer operator. Their IBM 360/370 computers were housed in gigantic, sterile, air-conditioned rooms that looked like the inside of the Tardis, but were infinitely less powerful than a modern laptop. While I enjoyed this job, the allure of cars attracted me and when Grandad asked whether I'd be interested in helping him establish a used car business for my parents, I jumped at the chance.

We worked hard to develop the business. We acquired some stock and made it ready for sale. Our most expensive vehicle was up for a dizzying £799! But there was something for every pocket – the average price being nearer £350. Grandad was officially retired and he found the work harder than he'd imagined. I was a young man, otherwise unemployed (having quit my computer job somewhat prematurely), and keen to make things work.

Initially, I found it hard to talk to people. My early sales attempts were awkward affairs. But, in due course, I found my style, got the hang of it and began selling. Soon we were selling enough cars to break even. Within a couple of years we recovered our start up losses and things looked promising. Then came a setback. Something happened which was totally outside our control: a worldwide oil crisis. Car sales ground to a halt overnight. Even more disastrously, the value of our £20,000 worth of stock halved. We were effectively insolvent and therefore effectively bankrupt! So much for becoming millionaires. Maybe we should have stuck to selling cars from home and not risked taking on premises?

Grandad, however, had seen it all before. Unfazed by this turn of events he said to me, "This is what we need to do: for the moment, forget the balance sheet. We must write down the stock immediately to its current value. We will then be able to sell it, because we'll be able to offer some very good deals. The new car dealers will need to get rid of their part exchange vehicles quickly, but there will be no buyers in the market … except you. You'll be able to buy new stock at rock bottom prices. You will then sell this new stock at historically low prices and make some money doing it. We'll claw our way back. We may need to be late submitting our accounts this year, but when we do, all will be well."

And that is exactly what happened. Two years later we had recovered everything we'd lost. All we needed to do now was move forward.

On one occasion, I was supplying a new BMW 520 to Mrs Mildred Pimlott. She was a strikingly beautiful woman, married to a gentleman with the unusual name of Sedley, and my hoped-for mother-in-law! Sedley and Mildred had a gorgeous daughter, Julie, who I was dating. But Mildred didn't approve of me and it was nigh impossible to win her over.

On delivering the car I took the new owner out for a spin, with Mildred driving, Julie in the passenger seat, me in the back. Mildred wasn't one for mincing her words. When we returned, she turned to Julie, blanking me completely, and said, "Just because I got this car from him, don't think it's going to change anything!" My efforts to curry favour by supplying the vehicle at cost price had failed. But hey, I had time on my side!

Near the centre of Long Stratton village were two other garages. One was a busy Ford dealership. The other was acquired by two likely lads who changed the name to "Stratton Motor Company" – too similar to our name for Grandad's liking. Some weeks later, keen to retain our distinctiveness, we changed our name to "Fridays" and, for the most part, we simply ignored each other. They seemed to be competent operators, however, and I was fascinated by the stock they sold. They focused on Jaguars, Mercedes-Benz and other "heavies", while we sold smaller, cheaper cars. I couldn't understand how they managed to sell them in the current marketplace, but they did.

Another dealer in the area was John Berry, ex-Lotus and a sharp cookie. We got on well and I enjoyed talking to him. One day I was admiring his premises and sensed the vibrancy of his operation. John asked me how much we made, on average, per sale. "Somewhere between £50 and £75," I told him. He raised his eyebrows. I asked the same question of him and discovered he made over £500 per unit. I couldn't believe it. It was one of those defining moments. Life was about to change. If he could do it, I could do it. We needed to make a paradigm shift. Thereafter I always bought cars I liked. Vehicles I would enjoy driving myself. Not only did I discover that we could sell them, but we could make a more than satisfactory profit. Of course, such an approach made for many a bittersweet moment. I remember the first Jaguar XJ6 to grace our forecourt. I didn't want to sell it, I wanted to use it myself! But somebody wanted it, so it had to go. That's the business.

So in the mid-70s the emphasis of our business shifted. We still sold a range of "bread and butter" cars, but now retailed slightly more unusual, heavier stock with the goal of making some money. One day we had an unanticipated visit from Roger Bennington, one of the two likely lads from Stratton Motor Company. He wanted to see whether we'd sell the business to him and if we were willing to discuss an offer. Whilst we had not made a significant trading profit after recovering from the oil crisis, the land and facilities had accrued in value and my family's £12,000 investment had risen to a whacking £50,000.

Roger wanted to buy and he also offered me a job as part of the deal. I was only 25. What would I do? If I'd taken that job, life might have turned out very differently. Which just underlines to me how much we need the oversight of the One who knows the future. We decided to sell, but by now my parents had acquired a new site on Mile Cross Lane, so we moved on and once again I turned my attention to building a new business in a new location.

Mile Cross was the former home of Valley Motors, a renowned operation at the heavy end of the used car market. The building we inherited was in a bit of a state, but the location was excellent. Slightly elevated, it could display around 25 vehicles really nicely and was a great place to do business from – something that became apparent within days of opening the doors. Even before we were through fixing the place up, cars began to sell – and faster than we'd ever sold them before. We managed to double our turnover whilst, at the same time, halving our advertising costs. As ever, I worked very hard and at the end of the year our auditors confirmed we'd made £75,000. Having made virtually nothing in the previous five years it seemed unbelievable. To put things into perspective, my wages at the time were £75 per week and the site had cost £41,000 to buy. In year two we made somewhere around £150,000. My parents, who ultimately owned the business, were enjoying surprising success.

ON MY OWN

Time moved on and, amazingly, I had managed to pull off the considerable coup of marrying the lovely Julie Pimlott. In due course, it made sense for me to buy the business from my parents, since I was the one running it. In order to do so I needed to borrow a whopping £200,000 from Barclays Bank. It was a big risk, especially considering the fact that by this time we had two small boys. Here was a new experience. Suddenly I was running the show for the first time. I had two sons and a courageous, but at the time, rather poorly wife. I had a house with a mortgage and £200k of debt to boot! I had everything to play for and, simultaneously, everything on the line. There was no way back. It was either sink or swim.

The goal in my eyes was simple: just sell enough cars to pay the bills. That was all I could do – keep selling the cars. Everything would surely work out somehow as long as we kept turning over metal. That was all I knew. I had no idea how many cars I needed to sell or how hard I needed to work. So I worked long and hard, every hour of every day except Sunday. I also made sure I saved some time at either end of the day for Julie and the boys. But other than that, every waking moment went into acquiring stock and finding a new home for it. I was so motivated to work hard that sitting on my hands for a day each Sunday was difficult, but preserving that day for going to church paid off in the long run. God blesses those who honour Him.

Ideally, before opening the showroom doors, I would have prepared an opening balance sheet, put together a budget for the coming year and calculated a cash flow forecast that I could update each month. Unfortunately, I didn't have a clue about any of those things! All I knew was how to buy cars, prepare them for sale, advertise them and sell them. So that's what I did. Week after week. Month after month. On the surface, things appeared to be going well. This is when God spoke to me, quite unexpectedly, about the future.

I was some weeks into this new venture. Sitting in my little office, adjacent to the showroom, wearing my favourite green anorak. My only possessions were a stainless steel Rolex day/date watch that I had been given and a copy of Glass's Guide used car values. I looked for all the world like the stereotypical Arthur Daley. I was alone. Then I heard a voice speak to me. It wasn't audible, but I heard it as clear as day and I'll never forget it. The Voice said, "One day you will be responsible for building a church for me for all ages from the cradle to the grave."

That was it. That was all. My immediate reaction? "No way! Absolutely not! That will never happen!" For a start it would cost hundreds of thousands of pounds, I reasoned. More like half a million. Maybe even as much as one million! In a typical lapse of concentration I mused on this. "How do you make a million?" I wondered. "In fact, how would someone make one million out of a single deal that they could use to build a church from scratch?" Not expecting a reply I was taken aback when I immediately sensed the answer. It didn't come from me. It wasn't an answer I would have come up with. All I knew was that in order to build a church I would need more than a pocket-sized used car pitch could ever produce. But God spoke to me and said this: "The way to make a million out of a deal is when that million is crumbs under the table."

Once again, that was it. The statement was left hanging in the air. No doubt about who had spoken it. It was a strange statement. It started me thinking. What if God gave me the ability to grow a business such that we had plenty of resources at our disposal? To expand it to the point where £1 million was loose change? From that day on my perspective on what I was doing changed. Everything I did was done with that goal in mind. God had moved me from "No way!" to "This could happen!" in the space of two minutes. Every pound I generated from then on was for a bigger cause. I had no idea where or when the time would come, but I didn't need to worry about that. God clearly had it all in hand. Sufficient for today was making sure I didn't let down the amenable bank manager at Barclays. But I had been given a priceless gift – *purpose*.

Ten months into the business I heard from the bank. They had noticed that the overdraft had reduced substantially and the manager was seeking an explanation. He wanted to see some accounts. Because he clearly appeared concerned, I became concerned. "Oh dear," I thought. "Who haven't we paid? Are there outstanding cheques waiting to be cashed? Have the bank made an error?" It was very unsettling.

Being a business with just one employee – me! – I had to investigate the matter myself. I took a dirty-edged A4 pad out of my desk drawer and began to list every vehicle I had purchased from day one. In the first column I recorded the price paid. In the next column I listed the selling price. Column 3 recorded the gross profit. In column 4 went the VAT. Then came a guesstimate of what I'd spent prepping each car. The last column contained the net profit. After that I calculated all I'd spent so far on wages, advertising and fuel etc., over ten months of trading. I added it all up on an ancient steam-driven calculator. It looked as though we were making an average of £20,000 per month! After earning around £70 per week for as long as I could remember this was absolutely incredible. Astonishing! The year end accounts prepared by those more able and suitably qualified than me confirmed the profitability. Thereafter the bank was happy and allowed me to get on with it.

What made them less happy on one occasion was me speculating on the foreign exchange market. I made a few small transactions to test the potential of trading currency. But then I took a big gamble and spent £175,000 buying US Dollars. I did it just before the market fluctuated and the Pound strengthened substantially. Fortunately, I sold them just before it peaked and still made over £70,000 profit. I was delighted. This was a profit worth having and from a single transaction. I was so pleased I went to tell my new friend the bank manager at Barclays all about it. His smile dissolved and the colour drained from his face as I did so. "Mr Dacre," he said gravely, "Your overdraft is to facilitate your business. We do not lend you money to trade in currency." Thankfully he never held it against me. And I learned another valuable lesson that day: don't tell your bank manager everything!

LIVING WITH PURPOSE

Despite the occasional impulsive decision like this, however, I continued to grow the business with the clear purpose God had given me always at the forefront of my mind. It was a journey, a steep learning curve, an adventure with many twists and turns, but I had a clear goal. In the book of Acts chapter 20 verse 24 the Apostle Luke writes about this:

"But none of these things move me; nor do I count my life dear to myself, so that I may finish my race with joy, and the ministry which I received from the Lord Jesus, to testify to the gospel of the grace of God."

In other words, life is worth nothing unless we use it to finish the task that God has assigned to us. Life is meaningless unless we are living for a higher purpose. If I can offer some valuable advice, it is this:

Find your greater purpose in life and live for it.

If your purpose looks easily achievable to you, then that's unlikely to be it. If you can't imagine your purpose coming to pass without some kind of divine intervention, you're probably on the right track.

There is great joy to be found in living out what you were born to do; being the person God made you to be and doing the thing that you are passionate about. As someone once said, "If you love what you do, you'll never do a day's work in your life."

Throughout the lifetime of what was to become the Lind Automotive Group, life was exciting. It got us out of bed in the morning. It didn't feel like work. We didn't just survive from day to day, we thrived. We were doing something with our lives and it had a bigger cause attached to it. It gave us purpose and a reason to excel. It satisfied our need to do something worthwhile and together we celebrated its growth and success.

The novelist Ursula K. Le Guin said, "It's good to have an end." We all knew that one day an end of sorts must come, but we put it to the back of our minds. I was the only one who knew it wasn't forever. But, even then, it wasn't really "the end" because God's ultimate purpose lay beyond – building a church that would honour Him and touch the lives of many in our community. This was the real vision. This was the underpinning, driving force. As DL Moody once said: "Let God have your life. He can do more with it than you can."

HOPEFUL PURPOSE

I'm the sort of person who is always looking forward, seeing where I can progress. Ironically, after all I've managed to achieve, I still don't feel I've arrived. One characteristic of a good leader is to celebrate the small wins. Unfortunately, I've never been able to do that. But I do look forward optimistically with hope.

Years ago, Tom Purves the MD of BMW used to host weekends for the proprietors of his dealerships. In 1994 Bob Gordon spoke at one of these events and talked about hope. He pointed out the difference between "hopeless" and "hopelessness". Hopeless is just an adjective. Hopelessness is a condition. We can all hope for the best, but we should never live in a state of hopelessness. Everyone was deeply challenged by the message. It was heady stuff for a bunch of car dealers.

Living with purpose gives you hope, because it means you can constantly look forward to the bigger, better things to come, and you don't dwell on the past, whether the past contains failure or success. But once we lose hope, we lose our direction in life. Thereafter we plunge into hopelessness.

When I became a BMW dealer, taking over a failing business, I had high hopes. I hoped we could turn the business around; hoped and prayed we'd survive; hoped we'd make some money. I hoped I wouldn't be a one-hit wonder. But this was all "negative" hope, as you can see.

Positive hope is grounded elsewhere. Founded in something that is secure. In something that cannot fail. In something that won't let us down. Just as God gives me a purpose, He gives me hope. As a Christian I have a sure and certain hope in the future. I have a hope that is not dependent or reliant upon me, but upon Him.

I came into relationship with God and found hope. Great hope. Certain hope. Sure hope. Once I lived without hope, but not any more. Today, I am hopelessly hopeful! Here's hoping that you will grasp this truth for yourself and begin to live a hopeful life, investing your efforts into a purpose far greater than yourself.

2
LEAP OF FAITH

"A man of courage is also full of faith."

– MARCUS TULLIUS CICERO

"To one who has faith, no explanation is necessary. To one without faith, no explanation is possible."

– JOSEPH CAMPBELL

Those not from a church background may find my perspective on faith and its role in business hard to accept. All I can say in response is that my faith is an integral part of who I am. It defines me. Therefore it plays a central role in all I do. Faith dictates who I am, what I do, why I do it and how I do it.

Frequently, faith appears illogical to others. I agree! The concept of giving away money and somehow receiving more back than we've given, for instance, is entirely illogical. But then many things about faith appear illogical on the surface. Yet, they prove to be true in due course.

As a man of faith, I believe that God speaks to me. Sometimes He will "plant" thoughts in my mind; pearls of wisdom that couldn't have been generated by me. God can give people insights that, if acted on in faith, can provide the key to unlock otherwise intractable situations. In this chapter I want to relate one such example. I was approached about taking over and turning around a failing business. But there was a big problem: it was haemorrhaging money and needed a massive cash injection to get it out of debt. I didn't have the spare capital to do it. But God spoke to me. He had a solution: simply go and ask the bank to write off the £1 million that they are owed. What? Surely not?

After just over a decade in the motor trading business I had turned my attention to property development. Although business was going well, I had concluded that rental income from investment properties could be a more stable, long term prospect than selling cars. So I set about investing our profits in buying properties and renting them out and this became my major focus for the next few years.

The venture went well and by the end of the 80's I had established sufficient equity and generated enough rental income to retire on. Then came another curve ball. There was a property market crash at the end of the 80's. The value of my properties plummeted and my nice friendly bankers wanted their money back. I had little choice but to batten down the hatches and try to weather the storm. Interest rates hovered at around 12-14%. Our saving grace was that rental income remained roughly equal to the quarterly interest charges, but it was touch and go for a few months.

During the aftermath of the property crash I received an unexpected phone call. It was the assistant to Mr Averill, the current owner of the Norwich BMW main dealership. He wanted to see me. I had heard of the Averill family, but knew little about them. I suspected Mr Averill wouldn't call without good reason and also that I was probably pretty low down on his list of people to contact, so I responded, "Yes, that's fine." Then added, a little mischievously, "How about next Friday?" (a whole week away). "Oh, Mr Averill was perhaps hoping to see you today," his secretary said politely but firmly. It was then that I knew the company must be in difficulty.

When we met later that afternoon I discovered from David Averill, a well respected businessman, that the company had mortgaged its premises at the height of the property boom. Worse still, its directors had bought a new and even more expensive site. During the subsequent property crash, both sites had lost a third of their value overnight and, consequently, their balance sheet looked horrendous. Ironically, it wasn't the bank who baulked at the figures, it was BMW themselves. Specifically, their Dealer Development Director, Jim O'Donnell – a man with a fearsome reputation for ruthlessness. O'Donnell had decided it was time for a change and had sent a short, to-the-point letter to David Averill. Unless the company could arrange a £1 million cash injection within the next 30 days it was curtains. They wanted their signage and all their cars back.

I talked the matter over with David. There was no obvious or easy way to get them out of trouble. The business now had no liquidity to buy, and therefore sell, cars. Outstanding creditors were demanding payment. The company was haemorrhaging £20,000 per month. The bank was unwilling to extend any further credit. BMW was about to reclaim all its stock and terminate the franchise agreement. At risk were the jobs of the management team and 50 employees. An audit suggested that the company's liabilities exceeded its assets by £1.35m. Personal bank guarantees were in place so, to cap it all, the Averill family house was on the line. Things could scarcely have looked more bleak.

David asked for my help and I agreed to give it – though at this point I couldn't see how I could make it work any more than he could. I didn't have a spare £1 million in cash to inject into the business, it was all tied up in property. But nevertheless, I owned the problem. The challenge before us was:

- How to keep the company afloat in the short term
- To persuade BMW to withdraw the threat of termination
- To keep the bank on side
- To keep the creditors at bay
- To return the business to profit

I decided to tackle the problem head on, so I asked to meet with Jim O'Donnell at BMW. We put together the finest corporate presentation possible, including plans to relocate the business to a new facility within 12 months, and indicating our willingness to "address" the balance sheet deficit (the one part of the plan I had no idea how to accomplish!)

All I could do was fall back on what I knew to be true: a scripture from Proverbs that had lived with me for years.

"My son, do not forget my law, but let your heart keep my commands ... And so find favour and high esteem In the sight of God and man." (Proverbs 3:1-4 NKJV)

In order to be successful we have to have help. The support of others is vital in business, as it is in life. But it also helps if God is at work behind the scenes. I was relying on the favour of God. I knew that He would come up with something!

The man at BMW was widely known as The Rottweiler. As

I entered his office he pointed to a chair without getting up or shaking my hand. Before I'd even had chance to utter a "Good morning," he launched into his assault.

"Sit down over there. Before you say anything, let me tell you that I don't like you. You flash property developers! You all want to own BMW dealerships. The property and motor sectors go up and down together, so as soon as the market drops you immediately want to cash out. On the basis that you now know where I'm coming from, I'm happy to listen to you!"

I was shocked. But something rose up within me. I looked this belligerent Glaswegian straight in the eye and with an edge in my voice responded:

"Mr O'Donnell, I have spent three weeks preparing this presentation for you. I left home at 3.00am this morning and have driven 200 miles to get here. Am I going to be allowed to make the presentation to you or not?"

I was allowed to continue. Half way through the presentation he stopped me.

"Listen," he said. "I've heard enough. You've got one month from today to sort this mess out. Here's my card. My home number is on the back. Give me a call if I can be of further assistance."

I'd met the biggest power broker in the UK retail motor trade and he'd given me some breathing space. I'd found favour again. We celebrated on our way back to Norwich. But we were far from out of the woods. There was no point pouring money into a black hole. What was more, BMW had indicated they would not support a bankruptcy and a new company being set up to trade under a new name. It would be bad for their brand and the local company's reputation. A week sailed by and no way forward materialised. A second week came and went and I couldn't come up with a solution. By the third week I was panicking, as we would soon be out of time. "What do I do, Lord?" I asked.

God answered. I awoke the next morning at 4.00am, sat bolt upright in bed and the most absurd thought entered my head. I knew it didn't come from me. It had to be divinely inspired. It was this:

"The company's bankers are your bankers. Ask them to write off £1 million of the company's debt."

That's brilliant, I thought. Then I checked myself. *No, wait a minute, that's ridiculous! Banks don't just write off a million pounds, just like that. They always want to be repaid. There's no way they will agree to it!*

Despite my misgivings, however, I just couldn't get the stupid suggestion out of my head. So much so, that over the next few days I had convinced myself that it was absolutely in the bank's best interests to do it! If they didn't, they would have to appoint the Receivers to wind the company up. And if they did that, then they would lose £1.35 million, plus £150,000 in fees.

It wasn't the future that was the problem, it was the past. The company had a poor trading history, so its borrowings had steadily increased. On-going losses were further eroding its strength. But if the bank would play ball, in the future it could become a great business to own.

Throughout this process BMW sent one of their senior officers to sit on my shoulder. It seems I had earned a reputation for using "creative" ways of achieving outstanding results, so I needed careful scrutiny and oversight! Gary Hickmott – a BMW company man through and through – had a firm grip on what would be acceptable, achievable and agreeable back at BMW HQ. In fact, the whole time he was with me, he repeated, ad nauseam, his mantra, "I think BMW would have a problem with that," which he repeated whenever I made any suggestion.

I told Gary I had found a way of improving the business's balance sheet by £1 million. We would simply ask the bank to write it off. He laughed out loud. Initially he thought I was joking. Then he realised I was serious and told me he thought it was an absurd idea. Nevertheless, I was determined to pitch for what I believed I'd heard God tell me. So it was that my newly appointed BMW friend and I went to meet with Barclays one Friday afternoon.

We outlined the position of the company to a table filled with grey suited senior bankers, first presenting the very sad balance sheet before moving on to my "debt restructuring plan". I said that the bank had two choices: agree to write off £1 million or call in the Receivers. We left them to ponder the situation over the weekend.

On Monday at 7.00am the Receivers were waiting outside BMW Norwich when the first employees began to arrive for work. They spent the next two days scrutinising the situation. Then they quietly and rather nervously advised the bank that they only really had two options: agree to write off £1 million or wind up the company asap and lose around £1.5 million after fees. On Thursday the bank called me back in. They too had realised that my "debt restructuring plan" was in their best interests. But they found the £1 million too hard to swallow, so they made a counter offer.

I met with the bank's Risk Director, Andy Cutter. He was a bear of a man; a 20 stone former international rugby player. He opened the conversation very bluntly. "We've had a good look at this Mr Dacre. We would like to see if we can agree something with you, but you will appreciate that £1 million is too much. We think the figure should be £750,000."

By this time I was in no mood to be denied. "I think you're negotiating," I told him. "I asked you for £1 million and you're offering £750K!"

"We're not negotiating," he insisted. "Let's consider it more of a discussion."

"No," I replied. "The stakes have changed. You have effectively reduced the figure by £250K. I'm now increasing it by the same amount. I'm looking for a write off of £1.25 million and I want it agreed by twelve noon tomorrow or I'm not doing the deal!"

Thereafter we did have a most straightforward discussion. A number of hasty side meetings ensued. Eventually Mr Cutter returned to suggest a gentleman's agreement whereby we split the additional £250K and he told me the bank would confirm everything in writing within 24 hours. We had settled on a debt restructure of £1.125 million. It had taken just seven days to arrange. Overnight we were in business.

The letter from the bank duly arrived. I faxed a copy to The Rottweiler. He couldn't believe it. He called and, typically economical with words, simply said, "Well done and welcome aboard." With that he was gone. For pulling off the feat I earned 60% of the shares of the business. David Averill was relieved to be informed that his house was no longer on the line and the bank would not look to him personally if it all went wrong. He had become a minority shareholder in the business, but he still had a home, a job, a share in the business and, more importantly, a future.

Initially, the thought of taking on a BMW dealership left me somewhat conflicted. On the one hand, having never succeeded at school and having only ever been a used car dealer until then, the idea of being a BMW retail dealer took my fancy. It would put me in a different league. Grandad had been a BMW dealer for a while in the early 60s. I wanted to follow in his footsteps.

On the other hand, I dreaded the thought of suddenly being

responsible for 50 staff. In my world, I operated with just a PA and then hired in professionals to do certain things as I needed them. The idea of leading and inspiring a large team was daunting. But my friend Bob Gordon encouraged and supported me. "You deal with the money side of the business and I'll deal with the people," he said. "That's what I do all the time." And that is ultimately what happened. Some months later I bought the remaining 40% of the shares for cash. In January 1993 we changed the name of the company to Lind and Bob Gordon joined the board to act as Chairman.

Thus, from a miraculous word of insight from God, the Lind Automotive Group was born. I hadn't anticipated it, focused as I was on property, but God brought it to me, thrust the opportunity upon me and showed me how it could work. From this unusual starting point began an incredible 14-year journey, during which time we saw the group grow from one dealership to twenty-three – having a presence in all major conurbations from Norwich to Gatwick.

If you are prepared to hand your business over to God and allow Him to become its CEO, I promise you will be amazed at what will happen. What would have happened if I had chosen to ignore what God spoke to me? What if I had stopped at, "No, wait a minute, that's ridiculous! There's no way..."

Right there and then I could have put paid to plans to grow an incredible business that would become an incredible resource, funding all kinds of worthwhile humanitarian projects. No business grows without its founder/leader taking a leap of faith at some point.

But instead of taking a leap of faith with some new marketing initiative, a new product or service, or some financial risk – take a leap of faith and trust God. You will never regret it.

"There are many talented people who haven't fulfilled their dreams because they over thought it, or they were too cautious, and were unwilling to make the leap of faith."

– JAMES CAMERON

3
LEARNING TENACITY

"Many of life's failures are people who did not realise how close they were to success when they gave up."

– THOMAS A. EDISON

"Do one thing every day that scares you."

– ELEANOR ROOSEVELT

In business as in life there is a need for tenacity. We must have sticking power in order to see ventures through to their logical conclusion; to push as hard as we need to see the results we desire. There is also the need to remain agile, able to respond to changing circumstances, and to take calculated risks when necessary. Sometimes in life you just have to stick your neck out and go for it! Make a plan – even an audacious plan – and put it into action; throw everything you have at it. Plan to succeed and not to fail.

On day one of our acquisition of the Norwich BMW franchise I went in to speak to all the staff and set out our goals for the future. I wanted to establish a, perhaps unprecedented, level of transparency, right at the outset, and made it clear we were all in this together. David Averill opened the meeting and then I spoke. I told the staff that I had acquired a majority share in the business and that I wanted to explain why it was necessary, before I outlined plans for the future . The last two years had been extremely difficult and so far, in the current trading year, the business had lost a further £250,000. This was unsustainable and together we needed to establish change. Costs needed to be trimmed down and, where possible, taken out altogether. Performance in all areas needed to improve rapidly.

I could see shock on the faces of many who, first of all hadn't had a clue about the real health of the business and secondly, hadn't expected such a level of frankness. I tried to keep things as upbeat as possible. "I have promised BMW a new dealership within twelve months," I said, "so we have quite a lot of work to do. You do your bit and I'll do mine. I'm good at what I do and I'm told you're good at what you do." I informed them that David would remain the boss at a day-to-day, operational level, and asked the staff to support him as we instituted strategic changes. Lastly, I told everyone: "I prefer first names rather than surnames. If we're in the presence of our bankers you can call me Mr Dacre, otherwise it's Graham. And by the way, you'll find I'm much friendlier than you may have heard! Thank you."

Thereafter we were up and running. The watchful eye of BMW observed what we did in the form of Gary Hickmott who, ever the company man, raised his eyebrows at the Mercedes Benz I was driving and said, perhaps for the one thousandth time, "I think BMW would have a problem with that." I hid the Merc and began driving a red BMW 840ci. I didn't want to upset him, his boss Jim O'Donnell (The Rottweiler) or anyone else at BMW HQ. Although

I had a history in the motor trade, the BMW management knew me more by my reputation as a property developer, so initially I was treated with suspicion and intrigue.

As we began to travel this road together, however, I soon realised the need for me to become more tenacious and determined if we were to see the positive outcome I had promised BMW. I enjoyed popping in to see how things were progressing. Pleasantness was available in abundance, but openness was in short supply. David, naturally I suppose, continued to run the business as his forefathers had done and he kept much, if not all, information to himself. Information was released on a need-to-know basis. I was less than happy when I realised that included me. It ran contrary to the openness and transparency I wanted for everyone at every level of the business. Such a situation couldn't continue. If the door wasn't opened to me willingly, then the current management would find me more than capable of lifting it off its hinges. That happened a few weeks into our relationship.

By this time I understood the importance of budgets and monthly accounting. I could read a balance sheet. In addition, I had developed a sixth sense when it came to spotting things that didn't weigh up. I could tell when accounted figures "felt" accurate and when they had been concocted via creative accounting. The first set of monthly accounts I was provided with didn't ring true. At the time I was busy, so I put them aside intending to review them in more detail later. They indicated we had made a small profit. When David sent me the second set of accounts, once again I felt a sense of unease. I couldn't see that things were turning around yet, but on paper it was a different story.

I asked the accountant to go through everything again from scratch and produce new accounts under closer scrutiny. When he came back with the figures the true picture emerged. During the first two months of my involvement we'd lost a further £40,000. At this point, for the very first time, I wobbled and had a crisis of confidence. It confirmed doubts I'd had about David. My first impressions of him had been accurate. He was a nice man. Almost too nice. And when he was hard, he was hard in the wrong areas. That afternoon I went for a drive by myself. I pulled into a layby on the A140 and thought, "What have I done?"

I wondered what would be the effect of Barclays calling in my personal guarantee against the business if everything went pear shaped. David was personally off the hook and I was very firmly on it. Yes, I had had the miracle of Barclays writing off £1.125 million. Astonishing! But I had still taken over a company with a deficit of £350,000 and we'd lost a further £40K. I was already in for £390,000 and that was without the closing costs. What had I worked so hard to win?

At times like this we need some kind of anchor; something to keep us steady. We need to fix our eyes on the original goal and apply tenacity to keep working towards it, despite the roadblocks and hurdles that are thrown in our way. I recalled that it was God's idea to get the bank to write off the huge debt – and it happened, just as He said it would. Surely that had not been for nothing. So quitting wasn't an option. There had to be a way through. I started up the BMW 840 that as yet hadn't been paid for and headed back home.

The next morning, aware that we needed to make top level changes and fast, I called Jim O'Donnell seeking his support for me to become more directly involved in running the business. He wasn't keen. In fact, he was anything but. He eventually agreed, providing that I was out within one year. Moreover, he insisted that Gary Hickmott would have to be involved in every major decision along the way. In the event, Gary and I got along tremendously well. With David's cooperation we removed an unnecessary tier of management. We also cut all residual ties with the past, recovering and selling a number of cars that were still being used by former employees who had long since retired. We prepared better budgets and looked at each department as its own profit centre, reconfiguring procedures and policies until we could see each area generating a profit, and with rewards being paid for achieving excellent results.

It was all basic stuff really, but David found it hard to come to terms with. We were dealing with his family, his past, his reputation. But establishing a better future was of far greater importance in order to save the whole thing from going under and many families being affected. For a period the figures would have to be the most important thing on the planet. If we didn't get them right it was curtains.

Near the end of 1992 David asked to see me. He applauded all we had achieved and admitted that he couldn't have done what I had done. But at the same time he felt I had usurped his position. It had been a tough year for him and he really wanted to branch out on his own again. I understood. He still had a significant shareholding, so I needed to think about an exit strategy for him. I asked him what he would need in order to start over. He told me he'd go away and think about that. Some days later he returned. He told me he had a figure in mind, but wouldn't actually disclose it as he didn't want to risk underselling his 30% stake.

Ultimately I had to take the bull by the horns. I prayed about it and felt that he would need around £200,000 to set up in business again. It was a tough call, considering that the business was still losing money and the balance sheet still indicated a significant negative net worth. But I felt God wanted me to accommodate him. When I told David what I was thinking he responded with emotion. Later he told me I had come up with the very figure he had in mind. A local solicitor drew up the paperwork and ensured the money was paid in a manner that was tax efficient for David. On my part, it was some years before I could look back and say it had been the right thing to do. But I was obedient nonetheless.

Once again, tenacity, persistence and staying power were needed in abundance. I now owned the business, but I had paid more than I'd wanted and the massive task of turning it around still lay ahead. I'd been enjoying my property developing and I hadn't really wanted to find myself at the helm of a car dealership again, but here I was. If there had been an honourable way out, I would have taken it, but there wasn't.

We persisted, however, and things consistently improved. So much so that eventually it made sense to relocate the business to better premises. We bought a new place in Ber Street when Kennings decided that one Rover dealership in Norwich was sufficient. Paul Lamacraft was the man from BMW responsible for helping to develop new facilities. He was as bad as Gary Hickmott when it came to reciting the mantra, "I think BMW would have a problem with that…". For Paul, everything had to be grey. The carpets, the fixtures and fittings, everything grey. I began to suspect he was colour blind. Once, when we were due to meet with Paul, we prepared a mood board. We put the board on show and didn't refer to it at all throughout the meeting. It clearly showed that we were intending to use bright yellow and purple alternate tiles in the WCs. I never mentioned it once throughout the meeting and could see Paul staring at it in horror. At last, when I got around to talking about the proposed colour scheme, I whipped off the two loosely fastened tiles revealing light grey ones underneath. Paul had survived. I was just having fun!

In January 1993 we moved into the new premises. The staff

were delighted. For the first time we supplied the ladies with business clothes. The men had to wear dark blue suits. We changed gear in more than one sense. It was a completely fresh start. All ties with the past had been severed. We had moved from the worst premises in town to the smartest and best. The name LIND appeared over the door for the first time. We looked the business and we did the business.

To kick start the new operation I repeated to the staff an old saying of my grandfather's – "*There's no taste in nothing*" – and added that therefore our goal for 1993 was to make £250,000. At first, no one believed I was serious. We had lost £250,000 in 1992. How could we possibly pull off a £500,000 turnaround? But we did. I told the staff this was our goal and, in addition, I would split with them anything we made on top of that £250,000. Suddenly everyone was interested in the figures and I shared them with the staff each month. At the end of the year there was an additional £40,000 of profit to split and we duly shared it out. Everyone enjoyed the fruit of their labour.

Brian Fawcett came on board as General Manager in 1993, later becoming Managing Director. He was a diligent and capable man, respected by everyone and known throughout the BMW group. He was to become and remain a great friend. Having persisted to achieve economies of scale in the business and further persisted to assemble the right team, we were now well positioned to grow. With Brian's effective management I was free to seek out new opportunities. I became responsible for securing new franchises, spotting appropriate sites and raising the required capital to purchase them. My friend, Les Brown, was responsible for project managing the development of wonderful dealership spaces (you'll read more of Les later when he and I have a near calamity involving a helicopter and a television mast!) Brian was then responsible for staffing each new franchise we opened and making each outlet profitable as soon as possible.

A thrilling period ensued where we grew the business and over a period of 14 years branched out from Norwich all the way to Gatwick Airport. It was an exciting time and we felt equal to most of our competitors. Looking back, what were the factors that made us successful?

- We had a strategy to only buy high profile, well-located land/buildings
- We made sure each new business was properly funded
- We created the most attractive customer environment we could
- We attracted and trained the most professional teams
- We motivated and retained key staff, creating an environment in which they could flourish
- We were honest and open with all our associates
- We treated others the way we ourselves would want to be treated
- We immediately put right any mistakes we made and honoured all our promises and commitments
- Above all, we adhered to our culture of excellence and upheld its values

CALCULATED RISK

At times we need to be tenacious by taking calculated risks. One can argue the case for business being scientific – consisting of certain principles that, when applied, will achieve certain results. To me business has always been more of an art than a science. I'm more interested in gut feeling; instinct; a sense of the right way to go; and whether something has the right feel about it. Without good instincts you can apply all the principles you want and still not achieve the desired results. That's why in this book I tend to speak much more about developing character than expounding business principles.

One of the reasons we were able to grow the Lind Group so quickly was the amazing support of Barclays Bank and later, Bank of Scotland. Another was our growing confidence on the property front. We developed good instincts for what would work. Les Brown was a great asset in this area and a constant companion as I viewed many potential sites for dealerships. Les has excellent town planning skills and over the years his advice has always proven to be 100% right. We never failed to secure planning permission on any site we purchased. Occasionally it was granted only after a planning appeal and other times we had to compromise our plans slightly or alter the design of the building, but otherwise Les Brown Associates was always victorious.

In Ipswich we bought a closed down pub and built a well located dealership for Land Rover. In Maidstone we acquired an amazing edge of town site occupied by a derelict hotel which was purchased and developed by Audi. In Tonbridge we acquired some farmland with an industrial allocation for Porsche. We turned an empty office block on the outskirts of Chelmsford into a stunning dealership to represent Volkswagen.

It was also in Chelmsford that we really struggled to find a site to accommodate a BMW dealership. There were many possible locations, but all were insufficient in terms of their size or prominence. There was only one site that hit the spot, but to date no one had been able to unlock it. The owner also had a Volvo franchise and would only consider a simultaneous sale of both businesses. This had put off many prospective buyers. We too were only really looking to accommodate BMW, not buy into another franchise that would need relocating before we could remodel for the German marque.

Whenever I was seeking to do business, however, I would always think things over carefully in order to establish, in my mind, what the man on the other side of the table would be looking for. I'd take those things as read. Thereafter I would look for opportunities within other aspects of the deal. It is helpful to know upfront, as far as possible, what are the non-negotiable elements and what is moveable. It is neither fair nor realistic to go into a negotiation thinking we're going to have everything our way.

After pondering the matter for several months I decided to phone the owner of the two sites, Michael Mimms, and talk to him about whether a deal of some sort could be struck that would give him, and me, everything we wanted. I asked where he was up to in his deliberations. I was sad to hear him say that he'd already made a decision. He'd found a buyer prepared to buy both sites and all that remained was to exchange contracts. Upon completion he was off to sunnier climes and a non-motor trade future. It appeared that he had agreed the price for both sites, but the contracts had yet to be signed, sealed and delivered.

I tried to push him. "Mike, I want to buy the Chelmsford site. I want you to come up with a figure that gives you what you want, so that it makes the sale of the other site irrelevant." Keen to deal I kept trying to get him to say, "Okay, if you offer me X then I'll accept it." But he wouldn't play ball. I hung on, like a dog with a bone, and he eventually conceded that if there was a conversation to be had, it would have to be quick, and we needed to do it asap. I rallied our management team as quickly as I could and we jumped in the car to drive straight down to the offices of Mike's lawyers.

Mike was a convivial old school motor trader. A warm-hearted family man with a great smile. He loved chatting with customers about all manner of things, but woe betide anyone who took him for being anything other than wily and shrewd. We eventually got into a meeting that lasted hours and we didn't even manage to table an offer. The conversation revolved around whether there was a price "tipping point" at which he would be prepared to split the sites. Mike looked at his lawyer and individually they pondered the matter for a few moments, trying to work out what the other was thinking. I tried to push them. They wouldn't budge. I was willing to deal at a price that would have made Mike an extra £150,000 for doing absolutely nothing. He would be foolish not to take it … but he didn't.

Things got to the point where there was no other option but to apply more tenacity and take a bit of an audacious risk. Mike asked for a break to discuss the matter more privately with his lawyer. They left the room together, but then the lawyer returned alone. "Mike very much appreciates you coming here today Mr Dacre," he said, "but he still wishes to sell both sites together and we have a buyer for both. My instruction is to get the matter concluded as soon as possible."

I looked at him. He was holding a blue folder that he clearly intended to work on as soon as we left the office. "Are those the contracts for both sites?" I enquired.

"Yes," he replied. "They are now in their final form. All the buyer needs to do is sign them if he wants to proceed. If he doesn't go through with it for some reason, I'm sure Mike will be back in touch with you."

I took a risk. "In that case," I said, "I'll sign them. I'm now willing to buy both properties. I'm here, ready to do the deal, so give them to me and let me sign them."

The lawyer stared at me. He couldn't believe what he was

hearing. "But you can't buy the other site," he protested. "You haven't even seen it. You'd be buying it blind!"

"That doesn't matter," I replied. "It exists doesn't it?"

"Yes, of course," he said.

"Well then, I'll buy them both."

Hardly able to believe what he was doing, the lawyer reluctantly amended the buyer's name on the contract. After all, he had been tasked with selling both the sites simultaneously to a single buyer as quickly as possible. Well this was quick! The deal was done. We walked out of the office with the contracts in hand. We had acquired the exact site we wanted, which was very good. Ah, but we had also taken on the other site and the franchise that we didn't really want. That was a problem. But all wasn't done and dusted yet.

Shortly after the deal went through I received a call from another dealer. "Graham, I heard that you bought both those sites from Mike. Is that right?" he asked. I confirmed it was true. "That's annoying," he said albeit amiably. "I really wanted to buy one of them."

"I only wanted to buy one of them as well," I put in.

"Really? Which one?"

I told him.

"Well I wanted to buy the other one!" he exclaimed.

I seized the opportunity. I had two sites and didn't want one of them. Another dealer wanted the one I wanted to dispose of. We did a deal there and then and I sold the site to him. He ended up getting what he wanted at a price that was agreeable to him. I ended up getting what I wanted and even made a respectable profit at the same time.

Tenacity, persistence and courage. Applied in equal amounts they will serve you well.

4
RETREAT TO ADVANCE
—letting go and leaving a legacy

"Some people believe holding on and hanging in there are signs of great strength. However, there are times when it takes much more strength to know when to let go and then do it."

– ANN LANDERS

It took me a little while to discover, but frequently it is only in the letting go of the old thing that the new thing opens up to us. As a believer, God requires me to trust Him for my future. Often radical trust is required. If instructed to, I have to be prepared, metaphorically speaking, to jump off the cliff – just as I did when I first became a Christian – taking a leap of faith; not knowing for sure whether I'll be caught or plummet to my death.

Equally, we take a leap of faith in knowing when it's time to let go of something and embrace something new. Everything has a natural end to it. There comes a time when we realise that one particular season is over and it's time for a new season to begin. Therefore there is a great power in knowing when to call time on something – even something great – and to quit while we are ahead. It comes time to move on. Be grateful for the past. Embrace the new.

After 14 fantastic years spent building the Lind Automotive Group, I sensed its season was coming to an end. We had done well. No, we had done really extraordinarily well. But all good things come to an end and I could see it was time. Many said, "Why stop now?" We had the world at our feet. Previously we'd had to go out and look for new business opportunities. Now they would just arrive in the course of the working week. On the other hand there were the tensions that arise as an organisation grows larger and you become more dependent on key leaders and employing those who know how to maximise the business for its shareholders. Others didn't necessarily see it coming, but I knew: it was time to let go.

Selling a motor business (or any business for that matter) requires good timing, patience and indifference in equal measure. The timing has to suit the buyer. Patience must be exercised in order to maximise the offer and not settle for a quick exit. But then you need to remain indifferent as to whether you sell or not. Switched on buyers can smell desperation a mile off.

I was also conscious that, as we grew in size, the number of groups in the UK who would be able to absorb us was shrinking. I had a conversation with Trevor Finn who was keen for me to know that if ever I was ready to call it a day he would be there with a sensible bid. I also had two meetings with Sir Peter Vardy. Nothing I was comfortable with materialised from either source.

Then in 2004 Martin Wheatley of Inchcape contacted me to say that they would like the opportunity to discuss a possible purchase of the Lind business. I had a lot of time for Martin and over the years we had done business together. He was involved when Lind bought Land Rover Ipswich and again when we acquired BMW dealerships in Malden and Ipswich. He knew his stuff and it wasn't often that people disregarded his advice on a matter. I enjoyed his company and appreciated his business logic.

Selling a business, especially a large one, is a sensitive matter. Most industries are really very small when it comes to news. Information travels fast and gets garbled like Chinese Whispers. Before long all manner of false rumours are spread. It was important, therefore, for Martin to sign a confidentiality agreement so that we could freely discuss all the sensitive matters without causing any problems. Thus began the conversation to sell Lind and move into a new season.

We had a false start. Martin arranged for me to meet their Chief Executive, Peter Johnson, and a couple of other senior executives at the RAC Club in Pall Mall. We met twice. At the first meeting I learned much more about Peter Johnson and his amazing career than he did about my business. At the second meeting I suggested that the business was worth much more than Mr Johnson was suggesting. One of his lieutenants was about to respond to me when Johnson signalled both his aides to be silent, holding his arms out horizontally like an aeroplane. He stood up, excused himself and told me he would be back shortly. He never returned. A couple of days later I received an email saying that he'd had a change of heart. I never saw him again.

I assumed that was that. Then the following year I heard from Martin Wheatley again, this time on behalf of Graeme Potts, who had taken over from Johnson. A far cry from the RAC Club, Graeme and I first met in McDonalds in Chelmsford! It was relatively empty when we arrived, but in due course we were drowned out by screaming kids. Regardless, Graeme made it clear that he wanted to do a deal and tabled an offer that indicated his seriousness.

There were a number of factors to consider. The amount to be paid for goodwill was one consideration. Then there was the sum of the net assets and how they would be valued. What would be included on the closing balance sheet and what would not. Of express interest to Inchcape was the method by which each balance sheet element would be valued. They had particular views on how new cars, demonstrators, used cars and service loan vehicles should be valued. Similarly car parts held in stock. Then there was the matter of debtors and creditors; corporation tax and capital gains tax to be assessed and agreed. Of great significance was the value of the commercial properties and which Inchcape were willing to buy, and which they didn't require.

At this point, a number of expert advisors became involved in the process to provide independent third party perspectives. William Jolly of Collier CRE advised on the value of our property portfolio. Several people at Grant Thornton, who specialise in giving tax advice, proved to be invaluable – especially when it came to drafting Heads of Terms. Mike Burridge of Grant Thornton stepped in to audit Inchcape's financial audit of the business. "We'll review their numbers and challenge them as required," Mike said. "It will be them on the hook and not you. We know more about the business than anyone. We won't let them get away with anything." And they didn't. Mike and his team were very thorough.

While all this was going on it had to be business as usual at Lind. Despite all the ensuing activity, I had no real assurance that the deal would definitely go ahead. Many a large scale acquisition has fallen apart after due diligence has been conducted. However, Lind Group MD Brian Fawcett and our Finance Director, David

Bonfield, were both astute individuals and had noted I'd asked for certain strategic information over previous weeks. They were looking at me questioningly and I had little choice but to level with them and secure both their confidence and cooperation. As expected, they were both professional and discrete throughout.

The group balance sheet needed to reflect all of the group's assets. With twenty-three dealerships there were a similar number of local balance sheets to examine. Brian was a man who advocated prudence, so he always retained pockets of money to cover the unexpected. He didn't like to suddenly reveal adverse situations to me, so he managed the finances well and covered any dips in sales, thereby presenting consistent figures to me, month by month. Now, however, we had to empty all the piggy banks. I asked Brian to send a memo to all our dealerships, asking them to identify any monies that, in hindsight, had been unnecessarily retained. In return for their cooperation, on this one occasion, we would pay the dealer principal a personal 10% bonus. With so many dealerships the figures soon stacked up and the result was a windfall of over £550,000 that was added to our assets. I didn't receive much thanks for this move, as most had previously indicated that all had been declared. Irrespective, I was pleased to pay out the best part of £75,000 in bonuses.

Brian and David were a great double act. Brian was the boss and held his cards close to his chest and, within reason, David was happy to play his game. I knew that both knew the value of setting some funds aside in the context of the group balance sheet, as well as individual dealerships, so I suspected there was still more to come. "You've got the lot," Brian insisted. "The cupboard is bare."

"No problem," I replied. "But just in case you can find anything else, I'm willing to give you and David 35% of it. 17.5% each."

Brian gave me one of his stares. David just smiled. I changed the subject. A couple of days later David presented me with some new figures. The resulting bonuses were substantial. They each did well, but the net assets had increased substantially once more.

The completion of the Heads of Terms was anything other than a simple overview of what had been agreed. It ran into dozens of pages and addressed the content, the spirit and the intent of the transaction. I enlisted Birketts law firm to vet the agreement and assist me in working towards its completion.

I was a deal maker and I was keen to deal. I had always made things happen. Thinking through the agreement I applied the same principles that I would if I was buying a property:

- What is the vendor asking for it?
- How much would I really like to buy it for?
- What do I think the vendor is really expecting to get?
- How much am I actually willing to pay for it?
- What would I pay at a push?
- What's my limit – my "top dollar" purchase price?
- And finally, how much would I have paid if I knew I was going to lose it?

More often than not I ended up dealing in the range of the last three. I have found that buying the best requires paying the top price. Owning the best allows you to ask for the top price when it's time to sell. In all business dealing, think big, stand tall and act smart. I put myself in Inchcape's shoes and pondered what they were likely to want out of this and what I was prepared to sell the business for.

Annette Whybrow of Birketts Solicitors represented me. Annette had been named one of the 50 most influential women in Suffolk. In retrospect it was easy to see why. Brian, David and I took the train down to London with her in order to meet at the offices of Inchcape's lawyers, Slaughter and May. We needed time to talk and go over the final details.

We arrived at Slaughter and May at 4.00pm. We hoped to have everything wrapped up fairly swiftly and return on a mid-evening train. It wasn't to be. We were kept waiting – and not just for a while, but for hour after hour. I was far from pleased. Was it a tactic? Annette kept her composure. We sat and watched the 9 'O Clock news. Then the News at Ten. Finally, Newsnight as well! I was ready to go home. Annette calmed me; told me not to worry.

When Inchcape and their heavy hitting lawyers finally arrived we had been drinking coffee for eight hours and I was in no mood for compromise. I wasn't going to budge an inch and Slaughter and May soon came to realise that the girl from rural Suffolk who they expected to be a walkover was more than a match for all of them. Annette was outstanding that night. They argued, they fought, they threatened. Inchcape tried to secure certain advantages. Annette beat them off.

There was one interesting moment. Inchcape CEO Graeme Potts came into the room where our team was encamped to discuss a technical point that could be argued two ways. Argued one way, it would cost us hundreds of thousands of pounds. Graeme knew where he wanted to go with it. I did too. David Bonfield our FD sat and listened. Eventually he chipped in with why he believed Graeme was wrong and the status quo should remain. Graeme eyed David cautiously, clearly thinking, "Tomorrow this man will be one of my employees." David reiterated the logic behind his thinking, all the time looking at Graeme and no doubt wondering, "Am I in the process of blowing my chances with this guy?" But Graeme was clearly impressed. He smiled, stood up and the matter was allowed to rest. David had gone up in his estimation. We'd won that round on his technical knowledge.

Remarkably, as negotiations pressed on, in the middle of the night Annette and I found our second wind. We were both enjoying this challenge and were energised by winning round after round, humbling the giants. Brian demonstrated his thorough knowledge of the business. David brought clarity and technical competence. Annette had complete authority on the legal aspects. I remained tough and unpredictable, still willing for it to go either way. Together we slaughtered Slaughter and May. By 5.00am we knew it and they knew it. It was then just a matter of processing a set of signature-ready documents. And all because they had left us sitting there too long.

But Inchcape were no fools and they had just bought a great group. The best privately owned motor group in the UK. They were just unable to score the additional wins I would have looked for if I'd been in their position. If only they had started the meeting on time they would have encountered much more goodwill and had greater time to achieve their goals. Annette Whybrow was an outstanding commercial lawyer and she knew her stuff. She knew exactly what she was doing and I was amazed at how she expertly established what she wanted and then achieved it. It was a joy working with someone far cleverer than me!

The Bible says that, "God causes everything to work together for the good of those who love God and are called according to his purpose for them" (Romans 8:28). I believed again that I was a recipient of God's unmerited favour. We had done our part – prepared well; worked together as a team; acknowledged we faced a formidable player; stood our ground and prevailed. God had done His part. As we left the offices to return home I reminded myself that I had gone into business ultimately to build a church. We did rather more than was necessary to generate the required funds, but then so many other good causes benefitted as a result. Above all, I knew, this wasn't the end of something; it was just the beginning.

THE DAY AFTER

I was relieved we had managed to get the deal done. It was finished. All signed, sealed and delivered. Oddly, there was no big celebration. No elation or champagne. Just firm handshakes all round, goodbyes and a palpable sense of loss. All I was sure about at that moment was that I had sold the business and tomorrow Inchcape would move in to protect all they had just acquired. At the same time there was no money, nothing to take home. The funds would arrive in three month's time. Everything felt new and unfamiliar.

Next came the task of telling each of the franchise principals what had just transpired. Brian, David and I arranged to meet them in Romford. I tried to pave the way with some positive news about bonuses. It didn't go down well. People always struggle with change – fact. Some took it harder than others. One or two said things I'm sure they later regretted. They needn't have worried. They were all highly regarded by their new owners. But it was difficult to keep the whole team on board during the handover. It's easy buying and selling bricks and mortar. Human resources are much more difficult to manage.

At the time I didn't understand the tears in the dealerships. I do now and I regret being the cause of them, even if I wouldn't have changed my decision. People had ultimately bought into and trusted me and I had let them down. It took them by surprise that I would cash up and sell out, as they perceived it. It wasn't meant to happen yet.

One conversation I wasn't looking forward to was with The Rottweiler, Jim O'Donnell. I knew he wouldn't take any prisoners and I really wasn't for being shot. But it had to come eventually. The resulting conversation was frank, long and tough. We talked everything through and I made sure Jim knew how much I appreciated him. He expressed disappointment at not being told. I explained that I had been restricted by a confidentiality agreement. The conversation ended with me telling Jim that I had tried to put myself in his shoes. I put it to him that if it was he who was faced with selling his business, asking himself the question, "What shall I do?" – what would he have done.

"Okay, what did I say I would do?" Jim asked, playing along.

"I would have gone for it," I replied.

"You're right," he admitted. "I would have done it too. You would have been stupid not to."

We remain friends to this day.

Extracting myself from the world of motor trading was no easy process. You soon come to realise that when you exit an industry, it carries on without you. Things soon move along. I took a call from the MD of BMW Financial Services. I remember thinking it was nice of him to call. He was obviously pleased for me. But no, he had only called to cancel my invitation to the World Cup in Germany that summer, since I was no longer in "the trade". He must have heard the disappointment in my voice. "You must understand, Graham?" he said. I did and I didn't. It was BMW's investment in the future. I no longer had one, so pragmatism took over. Other manufacturer contacts chose not to return my calls. This was a new world. One that I was quickly being excluded from. I did have a few new friends, but sadly they were only in the local media or fronting investment banks.

Later that day I went to visit my favourite BMW dealership in

Norwich. This is where it had all begun. I had to retain a firm grip on my emotions or I would have ended up crying too. The staff had been knocked for six. It wasn't the fact that I had sold out, they told me, it was the timing. This became a familiar theme I was to hear dozens of times over. "We just didn't expect it now."

The media questioned me about how I'd managed to be so successful in building, in their words, this "empire". I told them I'd used other people's skills, borrowed other people's money and bought and sold other people's products and assets. It had been a wonderful 14 years, but now I was looking forward to a new challenge; a new adventure. And I couldn't wait to begin.

THE PROBLEM OF WEALTH

Some may scoff at this comment, but one of the downsides of becoming wealthy is being able to have whatever you want. Imagine being a top Premiership footballer and earning so much money that you could buy a new Ferrari every week. You would soon get fed up of picking them up. But when I sold the Lind Group business I did treat myself to a couple of new cars.

Years ago, when I couldn't afford a particular car, like others I would dream of owning one. As a young man it was the new Jaguar XJ6 4.2 litre. They had one in the window of Drake and Fletcher in Maidstone in 1968. Walking from town I would stop and stare at it. In Regency Red with a tan leather interior it was, without doubt, the most beautiful car I'd ever seen. One day, somehow, I was going to drive one. My ambitions didn't extend beyond a drive. Owning one seemed out of this world. Forty plus years on I am still hoping to stumble across a perfect original. Time will tell.

What absolutely did it for me though was a visit to London in the early 90's. The flagship Mercedes Benz dealership was opposite The Ritz. On display was a Mercedes Benz 600, initially owned by John Lennon. He had then sold it to George Harrison and later it was used by The Supremes to tour America. Upon its return to the UK it was bought at auction by someone else before eventually being shipped back to the Mercedes Benz factory in Stuttgart, where it was stripped and refurbished to look as it did on the day it was delivered to John and Yoko. It was a Pullman – the long wheelbase limousine version, with a division and a sunroof over the rear compartment that seated four passengers, face to face. It was finished in ivory with a black velour trim and had a Radiomobile 8-track player and a Phillips EP45 record player in the back! I had high hopes and every intention of buying it back then. I made the owner an offer of £75,000 for it. He was polite, but the car was not for sale.

When I sold the business, I first of all bought myself a new Ferrari 430 Spider F1. The 430 remains one of the most usable supercars of all time. Then I managed to locate and purchase Lennon's old 600 Pullman. By this time it once again needed a bit of love and attention to restore it to its former glory. But now it looks just as good as it did the day I first cast my eyes over it. It cost rather a lot of money, but at the time I had more money than sense.

Another downside of being wealthy is that people constantly assume you want to give it all away. Regretfully, this has made me guarded in my friendships. Frequently people befriend you only because they are secretly hoping you will wave your magic wand and help them in some way. I hate to give people false hope, so I try to be careful. I don't want to allude to the possibility and unintentionally raise someone's hopes. Being able to meet the needs of others certainly makes you attractive, but it can also help put you in a box. Even the most genuine of people have to check their motives for seeking your company.

It's understandable, but it has also made me cautious. I love to give, but I also want to be strategic in doing so. You can't support everything.

THE NEXT BIG THING

It was 1980 when I heard God say He wanted me to build Him a church for all ages, from cradle to grave. Often the timing to start didn't seem right, for one reason or another. It wasn't until we thought that perhaps it would never happen that suddenly the timing was right and it made sense to open the doors of Today's Lifestyle Church, or TLC as it is affectionately known.

Pioneering a church from scratch is no walk in the park and a whole new adventure unfolded with many challenges – much of which must be saved for another book on the highs and lows of church building. Some came along to see what was going on, only to decide it wasn't for them. Others immediately grasped the vision of establishing a new, contemporary style church and were excited by it. I will be eternally grateful to Rev Muriel Shelbourne for her encouragement, guidance, wisdom and counsel in the months before, and after, the church was established. Similarly to John and Dodie Davies, who laboured alongside us for the initial two and a half years.

Often when a new church is planted, it attracts Christians from other churches who, perhaps dissatisfied with their current church, are looking for something new. This is inevitable, but I wanted TLC's main focus to be the un-churched. To reach out to those who had no connection with church and were likely on a journey to discovering whether, in fact, they even had a faith at all. I believe in the power of God to transform people's lives, set bound-up people free and heal the broken. These are the people we want to reach out and minister to. As a church we communicate a message that is relevant for today. Looking out for and caring for one another as a family is a high priority. We teach life principles and model situation-changing faith. In short, we are a "life transformation centre".

Many of my best friends are not Christians. My un-churched friends are mainly the ones I have chosen to do life with. Typically, I tell them that based on their current disposition I am concerned about whether they are going to make it into Heaven. In return they joke with me about getting them a pass or using my connections to get them in.

My friend Mike Adcock typifies the person TLC wants to reach. Mike is an amazing craftsman, a highly skilled builder who I've known and worked with for over 20 years. All that time he has had to listen to me telling him about my faith. Recently he needed my help in orchestrating the buying of a plot of land for him. I was glad to help. He asked me what he could do for me in return. Ask anything he said.

"Anything?"

"Yes, anything at all…"

I told him I wanted him to come and visit TLC on ten consecutive Sundays and we'd call it quits. He agreed. On week three Mike grabbed hold of me for a word. "Graham, I want you to know I'm not coming ten times," he said. "I'm staying for good." I smiled. I asked him why, if he enjoyed it so much, which he clearly did, he'd never come to church before. His answer amazed me. He was simply embarrassed and worried about what his friends would think. That was it. That's when I knew we were on the right track. We were building a church that the average man on the street would not be embarrassed to attend. Mike freely admitted he was still on a journey with his faith and wasn't too sure where he was at with it. But that didn't matter. TLC is a church for the un-churched. A safe place where people can discover God for themselves.

LETTING GO. LEAVING A LEGACY

Several years on TLC is a growing, thriving community with a purpose. It has great facilities funded by the profits of a motor trade business and provides a full time challenge that occupies most of my time and energy. It is an adventure I could never have started unless I had made the decision to let go of the past.

Often, the only way we can move forward is to let go of what we have. We appear to retreat, but actually we are advancing. I don't think God believes in retirement. In the Bible, many of his best leaders didn't come into the main purpose of their life until they were well beyond middle age. If we put our lives in God's hands then we never pass our sell-by date. We still have new things to learn, new goals to accomplish. I am still learning; still looking forward; still hopelessly hopeful about the future. The main goal of my life now has become to leave a legacy for the future. Not a financial one. But a legacy of changed lives.

"We can't be afraid of change. You may feel very secure in the pond that you are in, but if you never venture out of it, you will never know that there is such a thing as an ocean, a sea. Holding onto something that is good for you now, may be the very reason why you don't have something better."

–C. JoyBell C.

A SELECTION OF PHOTOGRAPHS TAKEN OVER THE YEARS

My grandfather was a really positive influence on me. He once told me, "There's no taste in nothing!" Later, after he told me off once, he said, "Well, if things don't change, they'll stay as they are!"

My grandfather Archie Friday had a colourful life. After selling horses he ended up with a remarkably tidy used car pitch. Decades later I had the same.

Never one to admit I didn't know something, I knew how to ask the right questions! Most often the answers filled the gaps.

I may have founded and developed the Lind group, but the reality is, it was others who built it. The key was employing those far more able than I ever was.

Someone once said you need two types of confidence: self-confidence and third party confidence. I generated a lot of the former!

Fridays – a corporate identity that has spanned five generations. FGS signs have looked after me for over 40 years.

My grandfather bought a mobile gas showroom and turned it into a mobile church. I loved swinging on its wing mirrors.

Stephan Philips has proven to be a great friend. Delia Smith was one of the few who has been able to attract his talent.

Some years ago I learned the power of silence, and that by using fewer words I achieved more.

Lind was the middle name of Dr Bob Gordon and in Norwich was the Jenny Lind hospital. In 1973 the licence plate "L1NDS" was available direct from the DVLA.

With the Lord Lieutenant of Norfolk, Richard Jewson – a constant source of encouragement and uplift.

With Mr David Gurney, a director of Barlcays Bank. Built in 1928, the building on Bank Plain was originally called the Gurney Bank.

Trying to look cool at one of our Harley Davidson stores. My son, Russell, deserves the credit for making a success out of them.

When I started out as a used car salesman I had to do the books. There was no VAT, no computers and no mobile phones in those days!

At RAF Coltishall. We painted the SOS bus. Later we raised £400K to buy two new ones. The original bendy-bus was last seen being wrecked on the *Top Gear* track.

1976, Fridays used car sales in Norwich, where we first started making profit. It was fun selling used cars in those days and I was good at it.

Receiving a CBE was amazing. It has made little difference to my life, but I appreciated the nomination and enjoyed visiting Buckingham Palace.

My first BMW dealership. We sought to provide customers and manufacturers with the best possible experience. As a result we had a great run.

The best Porsche ever – the 1973 2.7 litre RS – and part of my collection, which embraces all the cars I could never afford when they were new!

The Mercedes Benz Gull Wing. One of the most beautiful in my collection.

Celebrating my 60th birthday at the Open Youth Venue with two of Norfolk's favourite people, John and Barbara Cushing.

Reed International, Maidstone, my first job. Computers of the 1960s filled a big, air conditioned room.

Picking up a new Mercedes Benz 560 SEL in Stuttgart, courtsey of my friend, Sir Kyffin Simpson.

I've been invited to No.10 on a number of occasions. It is quite surreal walking up the stairs past the pictures of all the Prime Ministers over the years.

People always ask me what my favourite car is. Without doubt I have enjoyed my Porsche 911s more than any other. I like them because they are quirky but very well made, like me! This GT3 has a dubious history!

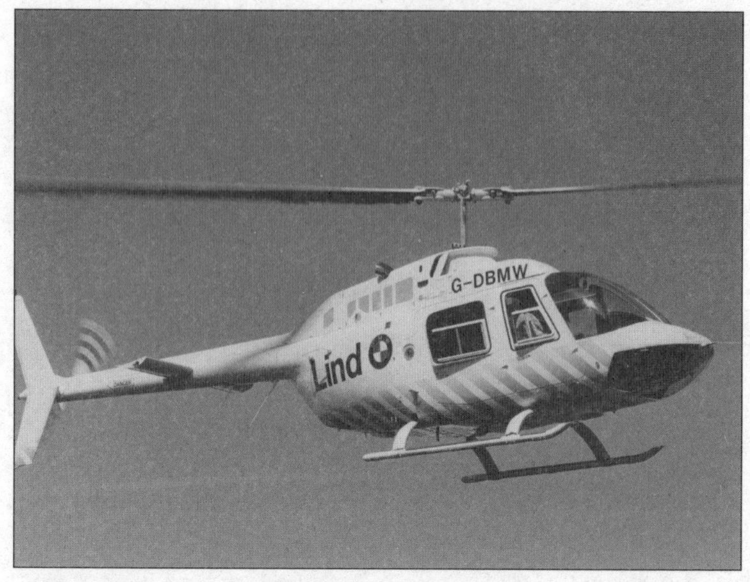

Julie and I were trained to fly by Captain Al Gwilt. He once told me that my flying style was "agricultural" compared to Julie's. I've never forgotten that!

When I married Julie, Norfolk became my home. It has been a great place to live, work and play. I've had a fantastic time here.

This proves I was a boy once and that I had some hair!

There have been some wonderful experiences over the years, but none better than flying myself around the UK. It was awesome!

I remember this picture being taken and thinking I had all it took to run the country. How utterly stupid I was!

The SOS bus project became a role model around the UK. I was glad to play a small part in its inception.

With my friend Gary Hickmott from BMW. I took all the risks and he made sure there were none to BMW!

Arguing with the indefatigable Nigel Pickover, Editor in Chief of the EDP. He told me he'd be happy to be my friend on the basis that any misdemeanours on my part would be front page news!

I don’t know where this last 50 years has gone!
I’ve had a really great life and there is more to come.

Some have said it was never going to be easy for my two sons. Both have successfully established their own identity and independence. I'm equally proud of them both.

I can remember driving this car and thinking, "What could be better than this? It will be all I ever need!"

5
THE BIG MISTAKE

"If you're not making mistakes, then you're not doing anything. I'm positive that a doer makes mistakes."

– COACH JOHN WOODEN

It is always tempting to read a success story and assume that the person has led a charmed life. That somehow they just got lucky. They were in the right place at the right time and everything just fell into place. This is invariably wrong on two counts.

Firstly, people love to write about their successes. It's easy to be wise after the fact. Easy to appear as though we expected a great outcome all along. People are less transparent about their failures. It's harder to admit we made a big mistake, misjudged a situation, got something badly wrong.

Secondly, it's very rare that success is not accompanied by failure. In business, you cannot have the big gains without some big losses. It goes with the territory. There is risk inherent in entrepreneurship, so sometimes you will win and sometimes you will lose. We achieve little by avoiding taking risks. And if we take a risk, then we have to accept the potential downside as well as the potential upside.

This is the story of one of my big mistakes and what I learned as a result…

A friend of a friend wanted to talk to me about a unique investment opportunity. He had become convinced there were opportunities to realise huge profits from little known and highly exclusive trading programmes. The monies that the banks raised from these transactions helped to fund the World Bank and the UN – to establish peace in war-torn areas and to help rebuild countries. Those involved in the programmes were of the highest order – international statesmen; world leaders; philanthropists. The profits made by the investors were astronomical sums, but were to be used to fund other humanitarian causes.

My friend had investigated these opportunities thoroughly. He indicated to me that participation was restricted to a very small number – trusts and individuals who were already seriously wealthy. Who didn't need the money personally. Whose lifestyles would not be affected materially, thus ensuring their discretion. Those who already had an involvement in humanitarian projects were ideal candidates because they would empathise with the aims of the programme. It all seemed very plausible. Scary, but laudable. It's easy to be wise in hindsight and see the holes already in the plot. But at the time it seemed like an amazing opportunity.

So how did one get involved with this venture? The key was meeting and building a relationship with certain key individuals. The "door openers" – the ones who could provide entry to this exclusive club.

For my part, I was only interested in generating large funds that could be used to underwrite various worthy projects around the world, with me acting as a distribution channel. With the monies we had made from the sale of our business as seed capital invested in the right place, we had the potential to generate huge amounts of money that could fund a vast array of good causes. I began to think about an effective way of managing and distributing the funds, assembling a board who would be responsible for viewing applications and interviewing prospective beneficiaries. Sadly, it all turned out to be a pipe dream; a complete scam. This is how it unfolded…

One day I received a call from a Canadian attorney. He was representing a major situation that would need to remain confidential and had been asked to make contact with me. He asked if I would be willing to see him if he flew over. He wanted to see the charitable projects we were funding in Norwich and report back to his clients. Thereafter he would let me know if there was a possibility of me getting involved. I need do nothing more at this stage.

In due course he arrived at Norwich Thorpe station – a sharp looking young lawyer; slim, articulate, well dressed. He was discrete, saying only what he needed to. He looked at all we were doing with great interest and asked pertinent questions. In due course he left as straightforwardly as he had arrived, thanking me for my time. I wondered what impression I had made.

Some days later there was good news. He called and said that while he couldn't make any promises, he wanted me to meet with a man called Alan Hunt. Hunt was a former marine and lawyer who was now giving his time to a major humanitarian project in Rwanda. "He may well tell you more," the attorney informed me. "You may find he suggests meeting you at his club. You'll like him. Ex-military. He's a good man and directly involved. Don't let his straightforwardness fool you. He has the power to get you into the programme. Call me after you've seen him. I'll be happy to help you in any way I can."

In due course Hunt phoned me. He was very accommodating. He had heard one or two things about the young people's projects I had funded, but wanted to see them for himself. That would also give him an opportunity to explain, first hand, how things worked. I could ask questions, as long as I understood the need for total discretion. I couldn't talk about it to anyone.

Hunt arrived one mid-afternoon in modest style, driving a dark blue Chrysler 300c. I had always considered them to be bad boys' toys and should have taken note. I was more amused by his registration number: USD5M. That too should have told me something. But Hunt was modest in his claims. He told me that he and various partners were involved in pharmaceuticals. He talked about another company involved in the production of biofuel and said he would enquire if they needed additional land for growing oil seed rape. I called various senior members of the local community on the off chance that some might be free for lunch. Subsequently Hunt impressed everyone around the table at the Last Wine Bar on St George's Street with his knowledge.

We began to talk in more detail. Hunt insisted I should not be put off by the unorthodox methods of the group he represented. They needed information presented in a certain manner for their systems. Later, as I started to engage with this process, I sometimes became irritated by what was being asked, but was told, "This is all normal stuff in the business. We deal with some of the biggest entities on the planet. Regardless of who they are, they have to conform. Where do you think Branson got all his money? We have the ability to perform. You have to do it our way or not at all. If you want in, let us know. If you don't, we understand."

Over the weekend I pondered the opportunity that Hunt eventually proposed to me. There was a high degree of exclusivity and also secrecy. It wasn't for just anyone. The minimum requirement for entry was an individual who had €20m "spare". Preference was given to those who had €100m. There was no "risk" to the investor, just a requirement that the funds remain static in an account for the next thirteen months. A complicated process would ensue where, in order for the bank to be seen to be trading these funds, they provided a "mirror" fund.

"We trade in your name," Hunt explained, "but using bank funds." He added, "You're not at any risk, but your money is tied up for the duration of the contract. You will receive an emission every two weeks. These monies are yours to use for humanitarian purposes. Don't go buying a helicopter or a plane! If you do, we'll know and the tap will be turned off. You won't be able to recover your position."

Hunt told me that he would send through the paperwork. He didn't push, but just said, "If you want to sign it, go ahead. It may not all make sense to you, but remember, the money remains in your account at all times, under your signatory control. You're not at risk. You may think this all sounds too good to be true, but it is true. We can make this work well."

What was the payoff? An investment of €20m would reap an incredible return of €2m, extended every ten trading days. It did sound too good to be true. Because it was.

Having got to this point, Hunt began to lay it on thick. There were certain dates allotted for entry into the programme. If you missed one, you had to wait for the next slot, maybe for months and months. He name-dropped some of the world's largest banks as players. He said that the banks leveraged these investment funds by up to 50 times their original worth. The profits would be enormous.

It looked like a no-brainer. All I had to do was put the equivalent of €20m in a non-depletion account for 13 months. It remained under my sole signatory control. All it had to do was sit there, quietly. I had no obligation to cover losses. There were no fees. The legal documentation was unusual, but there were no obligations other than to sit tight; to spend the proceeds on charitable causes. Where was the risk?

The following week I happened to be speaking at a breakfast meeting in a hotel in Bath. Hunt came along and brought one of his two partners. I was introduced to Arthur Ford-Batey. The plot thickened as Hunt and his associates appeared ever more plausible. I actually believed that between them, they had access to a system for releasing huge funding for good works. I wanted to believe them. If it could work and I could benefit the lives of many others without risk, then why would I not want to go ahead?

A good friend of mine, Tony Bunker, was there with me at the hotel. Tony is a very bright man who had been a HMRC tax inspector and a friend for many years. He has perhaps the most illegible writing I've ever seen – really miniscule. Tony left the revenue to become a lawyer. I asked him why he wrote so small. He told me that as a tax inspector he became accustomed to reading other people's scribbled notes upside down whilst conducting investigations. When the gamekeeper turned into a poacher and began defending others, he wanted to make sure that no one could ever do the same to him! This day, however, it wasn't hard for me to read what Tony was thinking. In fact he told me what he felt in no uncertain terms: "Who are these guys? What they are saying is rubbish! It's absurd!"

Sadly, I didn't heed his warning. I persevered. Hunt sent me draft documentation. Tony told me straight that I shouldn't touch these people with a barge pole. But what do lawyers know? There was no risk as far as I could see.

Eventually I was introduced to the final member of the trio. George Katcharian was described as a man with a huge intellect who spoke at least eight languages. He was the brains behind the system. The trader. The one who connected with the banks and accessed the alternative trading screens. Ford-Batey was clearly in awe of him. In their business Hunt fronted the partnership, Ford-Batey dealt with the paperwork and Katcharian conducted the financial transactions. The banks earned substantial amounts from their activity, as did their investors. The World Bank got what it needed. The UN could fund its activities. Economic collapses were avoided. The world was kept afloat.

Looking back, you can see how stupid I was. Me too! But they had done their work patiently and thoroughly. I had been programmed well and drawn into an "unprecedented opportunity to benefit others". So I wanted to go all in. I had always done that. Time and again over the years I had put everything on the line in order to grow. The bigger the risk, the more I had enjoyed it. I wasn't risk averse. So I was their perfect punter – someone who took good advice but who, when the moment called for it, was prepared to ignore it. A man who wanted to do good. I had around £40m I was prepared to put in, as agreed, for 13 months. I told them so. They knocked me back. "We're not sure we can handle all that at this time. We'll come back to you…"

Eventually Hunt came on the phone to me. He said they'd discussed the matter and would be able to bring in my £40m, but it would have to be done in two separate tranches and in Euros. He told me the partner bank on this occasion was Credit Suisse in Zurich and said they could bring me in immediately to the tune of €15m – just under £12m at the time. "Let's get going with this smaller amount," Hunt said, "and I'll do everything in my power to accommodate the larger amount in the next programme."

Everything was agreed. Paperwork signed. I would invest in Euros. I cashed a Sterling Reserve Bond for £12m. €15m cost me £11.9m and I put the balance in my current account. By the end of the day the money was sitting in a Euro account waiting. I had been successful. But the feeling of success was to be short lived. We were about to be conned. I was about to lose a small fortune.

Hunt came to see me in Norwich again. I had grown quite fond of him. Nothing was too much trouble and we'd struck up a good relationship. We'd enjoyed a number of meaningful conversations. He had won my confidence. I felt as though I'd known him for much longer than I had. Any doubts I had dissolved as he graciously worked through any remaining questions. We had dinner together, then he told me he had something he needed to tell me.

Here was the sting. Due to issues currently affecting the UK and European banking system, the programme needed to temporarily move its trading platform to Zurich. We had to take on board certain European banking requirements that were mandatory and therefore affected every new entrant into the programme. To proceed would require me to make a "leap of faith". If that wasn't something I felt I could do, they would understand. But the monies now had to be remitted to a "system" account. On receipt, they would immediately initiate the trading programme. Monies would be credited back to my account, which I controlled, in a matter of 4-8 working days. Upon receipt we would be invited to attend a meeting at Credit Suisse to sign contracts. Hunt played it all down. It was a pain and an inconvenience but nothing more, he assured me. Just a formality and we would be up and running.

"In respect of the other £30m," Hunt said, "we will get you in

ASAP. First you need to decide on the €15m – whether you wish to proceed or not. We have taken the liberty of amending the contract to reflect the new arrangement. Perhaps you can check it out? You will need to sign it first and we will then countersign it. Once both parties have signed we will send you Appendix A. We don't issue our bank details to any third party until they have unequivocally confirmed their intention to proceed."

Of course, this was not what we had agreed, but once again it was plausible. It was a year when there had been a major banking crisis and things were changing fast. The distress in the banking system was obvious and the reasons given were credible. I had confidence in Alan. To date he had always done what he'd said he would do. He also signed a personal guarantee which meant he too was putting everything on the line. They all did. Tony Bunker told me that if they'd signed guarantees, they'd be mad not to perform. So I went for it.

I spoke to Tony again. He remained far from sure. He said I could still do a lot of good with £12m, so ultimately advised against going ahead. I sensed he would. It was his job to be cautious. But I ran with it. Signed the papers. Faxed them off. I received Appendix A back in due course. It was then that I noticed a new name on the paperwork. "Ian Yorkshire" had been added in there. Who was he? Another associate in this mysterious operation no doubt. It was too late to worry about it now. I gave instructions for the €15m to be transferred to the new account and kissed goodbye to it … forever. I had been robbed, but it took some time before the full, awful realisation dawned.

Next came the stalling tactics. I had authorised the wire transfer on a Friday. Hunt and his associates told me on the Monday it had not arrived. The same thing happened every day for the rest of that week. The following Monday they confirmed it had finally arrived, having been exploited for one week for the bank's gain. All the while my own bank assured me that the funds had been transferred the same day. It wasn't a good start.

Four working days soon passed. As did eight. Nothing happened. No invitation to the bank in Zurich materialised. Hunt and co made a number of reassurances. Every promise went unfulfilled. Each time there were reasons and excuses. They were waiting for someone to get back to them. Someone was out of town. All three men were in touch with me, all making excuses; each covering for the other.

Then came another twist. An apparent falling out between the team of three. Hunt said he had upset his partners, but he wasn't giving up. He expressed his apologies and said it was all very embarrassing.

I kept asking about the meeting with Credit Suisse. Eventually I managed to extract a meeting date and flew out to Zurich with Tony. The person we were supposed to meet didn't turn up. Instead we met another character who was involved in the scam, Cemal Esmene. Our meeting in a hotel lobby was a farce. There was no meeting with the bank and no €15m returning into my account. They were still working on that.

I persisted in asking for a meeting with the three main players. They promised to come and meet with me. The first time only Hunt turned up. Later the others came too, but there was still no news. Just nonsense and excuses. That was when I first realised I was in trouble. The legal documentation was useless at best. I did my best to keep hope alive, day after day. But day after day there was no sign of the money. The days tuned into weeks and I knew...

Looking back, I still can't understand why they came back to Norwich to meet me again. They had the €15m. Perhaps they were hoping I would continue with the rest. Then they'd really clean up. They could take me for a further £30m.

As soon as my suspicions were aroused I began keeping an electronic transcript of everything: every conversation, every promise, every excuse. I kept mobile phone texts. I copied emails. Over the months it became a substantial document. Ultimately it provided vital evidence of everything that had been done. I felt sick. I felt utterly stupid for being sucked in. There had been tell tale signs all along, but I had overlooked them. From time to time I would tell my sons the latest. They didn't say much. They felt for me. They knew. Julie too.

Over the months Hunt continued to travel to Norwich to see me. It was oddly reassuring to see him. He hadn't just absconded. While he was still around there was still hope. Ultimately, however, I began to turn up the heat. Slowly at first, then more directly, suggesting I would involve the Police. Hunt told me point blank that they wouldn't be interested. This was a commercial transaction gone wrong. If it went to court, I would lose. Plus it would take years to sort out. He advocated patience. "It wouldn't be wise to fall out with us," he said, ever the confidence trickster. He claimed that the more we upset his partners, the more difficult it would become to resolve the matter. Eventually I told Hunt I'd made a statement to the Police. I'm not sure he believed me. Later I told him I'd put the matter into their hands. He said if that was the case he'd be happy to help them with their inquiries.

The final time Hunt and I met was in my office. I said he should expect a visit from the Police in due course. It was all in hand. Not a matter of if, but when. I told him he would end up in jail. For the first time he realised I was serious. He gazed at me for a few seconds and then broke down and cried. There was no remorse for ripping me off, just tears of regret for what he'd done, for being caught, and because he knew the situation was irreversible. Others had taken the money. They were unlikely to return it. He perhaps regretted his involvement. But there was no way out. He knew where he would end up – and he was right.

THE TRIAL

The handling of the matter by Norfolk Police was thorough and outstanding. With limited resources DC Christopher Gay and his team pursued the criminals in the UK and abroad. The investigation was kept under wraps, since it could prove to be wide ranging in its scope. Homes were raided and computer equipment seized. Those considered a flight risk were held on remand.

In the first round, six men were charged and brought to trial in the High Court in February 2012. Most were charged with fraud; others with money laundering; several with both. I met Ford-Batey and Hunt outside the court. Hunt gave me a confident smile. As well as the familiar trio, in the dock that day were three other men I'd never met – all part of the operation. Until now they had cleverly remained behind the scenes. The jury found these three not guilty and they walked free from the court with an obvious air of relief. They should have gone to prison.

The trial lasted four months and involved 14 lawyers. I endured two days of cross examination by QCs acting on behalf of both prosecution and defence. I wasn't up for saying the things that the defence QC clearly wanted me to say. In the end, everyone seemed satisfied with my performance. It wasn't enjoyable, but it had to be done.

The trial concluded at the end of May. I sat with my family in the public gallery to hear the verdicts and returned again for sentencing. Hunt was found guilty of two counts of fraud. He had defrauded me and also a church in Germany at the same time. He received a five-year sentence for fraud and a further four years for money laundering. Ford-Batey received five years for fraud. Ian Yorkshire, whose name had mysteriously appeared on the legal paperwork, was found guilty of defrauding me and laundering the money through his personal account, for which he received five and six years respectively.

George Katcharian – the "finances man" of the scam team – proved more elusive and harder to bring to justice. An international warrant was issued for his arrest. But he was no fool. He clearly knew the law in various places around the world and seemingly knew where he could fly to and where to avoid. In his mind, he could easily outwit the Norfolk Police. But, all set to celebrate Christmas 2011, Katcharian purchased an airline ticket from Hong Kong to Zurich and the Police heard about it. They figured he planned to drive to Germany to spend time with a known associate. The German Police staked out the property. When he arrived there was no way for him to escape. The Police even impounded his Christmas presents. In due course he was tried and convicted for the part he played in defrauding both me and the German church.

When it was all over there was no elation. No celebration. Just an enormous sense of relief. It had taken four years to complete the investigation. The criminals were found guilty. It would now be possible for Norfolk Police to pursue the men for the recovery of the monies under the Proceeds of Crime Act. A matter that is still on-going at the time of writing.

During the trial Julie and I received many calls, cards, emails and letters of support from the most unexpected of people. All of them were so kind. We were also perhaps surprised by those people we didn't hear from. Though speaking to one or two of them afterwards, they admitted they'd had no idea how to cheer me up.

Once I realised we had been defrauded in 2008 I did a number of things. First of all I wrote off the money. We had made a number of good investments over the years. This just happened to be one that produced a loss – a really big one! Then I determined to do several other things that I will summarise in a moment.

If you are an entrepreneur you will have made mistakes. If you've never put a foot wrong in building your business, you are either completely unique, a total one-off and should celebrate the fact, or you have never taken a risk! The odds are overwhelmingly stacked in favour of the latter.

The most important thing about mistakes is simply that we learn from them. Mistakes happen. Mistakes are inevitable. Yes, they may make us feel stupid. But the only really stupid thing is to make the same mistake again. You may never make a mistake of the same magnitude as me, but the following advice applies nonetheless:

1. *Learn from the mistake.* Be better prepared next time. As George Bernard Shaw said, "Success does not consist in never making mistakes, but in never making the same one a second time."
2. *Don't punish yourself.* I made a decision not to pay twice for my mistake. It happened. I wasn't going to torture myself emotionally.
3. *Don't let it ruin your life or sap your confidence.* Okay, so you made a mistake. Now it's time to get over it and move on. One mistake, however bad, doesn't cancel out all the years of success.
4. *Don't give the matter undue head space.* I refused to let the matter play on my mind and I didn't think about it unless I had to – such as when Norfolk Police called to discuss some

aspect of it. Apart from that I refused to allow it to dominate my thinking.

5. *Carry on as though it never happened.* Life had been good until the Big Mistake. It was going to be good again. And it was. Success is not just something that happens to you, it is a state of mind. Get back on the horse. Get going again. Stay positive.

As the singer Johnny Cash once said, "You build on failure. You use it as a stepping stone. Close the door on the past. You don't try to forget the mistakes, but you don't dwell on it. You don't let it have any of your energy, or any of your time, or any of your space."

Sound advice.

PART 2
LIFE LESSONS FOR WOULD-BE ENTREPRENEURS

6
THE IMPORTANCE OF MENTORS

"Just about ANY personality trait or skill can be learned: simply find it in someone you know and copy it. Then watch what happens."

– **STEVE GOODIER**

"Spoon feeding in the long run teaches us nothing but the shape of the spoon."

– **E. M. FORSTER**

People often ask me what I think are the most important qualities that an entrepreneur needs to possess. Potentially there are lots of answers; lots of characteristics, all important in their own right: perseverance, risk-taking, the ability to bounce back… But to me, perhaps the two most important, inextricably related, qualities are:

- The ability to learn
- The good sense to seek wise counsel

It strikes me that the majority of the most successful entrepreneurs are lifelong learners. Few are those who have made their way to the top by being hard-headed and arrogant in their single-mindedness, refusing to listen to others' advice. On the contrary, they tend to be open, humble and receptive to all good input. And they are willing to be flexible – to adapt to new learning and act upon it.

I have tried to remain a lifelong learner. There are always new things to learn, new challenges, new horizons to explore. It prevents life from becoming boring. But I have also been blessed to have been able to learn from some great mentors – men who formed an important part of my life and whose example had an impact upon me, changing me as a result. In this chapter I'd like to mention some of them and what I learnt from them.

GRANDAD – THE SPIRIT OF ENTREPRENEURSHIP

It was my grandmother who first came to faith in the Salvation Army. The obvious transformation in her life was apparent and this impacted my grandfather. It wasn't long until he too came into a relationship with God. Grandad and Grandma embraced a new lifestyle, rather different to that which they'd known before, and as a result their six children grew up in a very different environment – each of them establishing, in different measure, their own relationship with God.

The family surname was Friday. Grace Margaret was the youngest of three Friday girls. Later she would train to become a nurse at Leeds Royal Infirmary. Attending the Assembles of God church there she would meet and fall in love with a handsome young man with rolls of "stepped back" black hair. She became Mrs Leslie Dacre in 1948. My mother.

Dad was a kind, gentle, selfless, God-fearing man. His own

father had died when Dad was just 14. Thereafter he had worked hard to support his mother and never complained. In fact, I never once heard my father complain about anything. It seems that he never considered he had reason to be anything other than grateful. His faith sustained him.

My grandfather on my mum's side was a colourful, resourceful character. He was my first mentor in running a business when we lived in Maidstone, Kent. He was a natural born salesman who could buy and sell anything. At the end of the Second World War he used his wit and charm to talk a local auctioneer into allowing him to "buy" cars from his auction, but not pay for them for seven days. He therefore had one week to sell the cars and make a profit. The deal was that if he wasn't able to pay for a car within the week, he had to return it, to be entered into the following week's auction. Few were ever returned and in time "Fridays" would become a well known brand name across Kent in the 50s and 60s.

As a teenager I was impressed by the fact that the business advertised on the back of Maidstone and District buses. Fridays had sites in both Maidstone and Gravesend and had more than 300 used cars in stock at any time. In hindsight, the business was years ahead of its time in its approach. The stock security system was considerably less ahead of its time, but nonetheless remarkably effective. The cars were stored in a fenced compound, within which several Alsatian dogs were allowed to roam free at night. To keep them hungry and awake they weren't fed until the next morning! I can't remember ever hearing of a vehicle being stolen.

Grandad was the principal, driving force behind the business, but increasingly his new found faith in God was demanding his attention. As soon as some of his sons were capable of assisting with running the business he would be on the road. He had a caravan, plastered with Bible verses advocating repentance and the downside of not being ready to meet your Maker. He was like an old-time itinerant preacher, but a highly mobile one. Grandad cut a picture of authority using a ringed BBC-style microphone to address the crowds of people that he attracted on village greens and in towns around the country.

Later he upgraded his operation, buying a redundant mobile "gas showroom" with expandable sides. After setting up this mobile church he would personally distribute leaflets to every nearby house, inviting people to attend his revival meetings. Once enough people in one area had responded to the call for salvation he established a local church there, appointed a pastor, then moved on. Grandad was a pioneer. Whether running his car business or spreading the word, he showed me how to pursue a goal until it was achieved.

Grandad continued to focus on his pattern of building a church in a particular location, then returning home to see how his business was doing. His boys were not as good at selling cars as he was. When he was around, good things happened. He had the entrepreneur's touch. When Archie Friday was in town, all was well.

Long before I knew anything about the business, Grandad's visits captivated me. His company always lit up a room. He drove nice cars, always arriving in something special. I recall elegant Rovers, a new maroon-coloured Humber Super Snipe that was later used to ferry around the evangelist Billy Graham when he visited Haringey, London in 1966. I remember a Mercedes Benz 280SE that he bought from the boxer, Henry Cooper; a supercharged Aston Martin Lagonda. I remember even more vividly the day Grandad suggested I drive him home in his brand new BMW 1800. That was fun. I was only fourteen at the time! I loved my Grandad. He was my hero. He still is today.

DAD – HARD WORK AND EXCELLENCE

One of the churches that Grandad built was in Corby, Northamptonshire. He oversaw the construction of the building himself (using voluntary labour). Once again he appointed a pastor and this time also my father as Sunday School Superintendent, before again returning to see how his business was faring.

The church has stood the test of time and in just the last couple of years I returned there and preached myself at its 60th Anniversary Celebration. There was a lady in attendance who used to take me out for walks in my pushchair some 58 years ago!

Mum and Dad established a small business in Corby, a retail pram store in the centre of town. In addition, Dad would personally repair and refurbish used prams. In past, more frugal times, the family pram would be used by all the members of the family before being retired. But then, with a new hood, apron and occasionally a new interior lining, it could be roadworthy once more.

Dad had a gift for restoring any pram to its former glory. Reupholstering them became very personal to him. He spent so long and did such a good job on each one that I can't imagine he earned much more than pocket money from doing it. But I remember that his customers were always delighted. He was a real craftsman and I was full of admiration for him. He was always very caring and supportive and worked very hard, asking for very little for himself. He taught me the value of excellence, diligence and hard work.

On top of these qualities Dad was always immersed in the Bible. At church meetings he would frequently read out loud a particular passage of Scripture that he had been reading. Some found this comical or quaint. But it gave me a quiet confidence in my Dad. He was grounded in his faith. It gave his life a firm foundation. I also learned from him the importance of being rooted and grounded in God's Word. It has provided my life with a similar foundation.

SIR KYFFIN SIMPSON – VALUING PEOPLE

One of the great privileges of being moderately successful is often finding yourself in the company of those who are even more successful. People who you could never otherwise imagine meeting. When we met, he was plain Kyffin Simpson. Now he is Sir Kyffin Simpson Kt CBE and deservedly so. To me he is one of the most remarkable people on the planet.

Kyffin was a motor trader, like me, but on an altogether grander scale. We met in 1980 when he was an international director of the Full Gospel Business Men's Fellowship and President of the Bridgetown Chapter in Barbados. Another longstanding friend, John Wright, had suggested that I make the trip to Barbados to speak at a men's breakfast there, when my travel schedule next made the logistics of getting there do-able.

Kyffin is one of the people I consider a lifelong friend. He is a tireless encourager. Whenever we get together he will invariably unpack my dreams and unfold my aspirations. Over the years he has encouraged me to seize many opportunities I might otherwise have passed on. "Go for it, Graham," he would urge. "You can do it. If you need help, let me know. I'll come in on it." I knew he meant it too. I was always aware that he was right behind me. He had my back. A true friend. If there is one person I've tried to model my life on, it's Kyffin. He imparted to me the gift of valuing others; of recognising potential and encouraging it to blossom.

Julie and I flew out to Bridgetown that first time not quite knowing what to expect. On the flight over I was seated next to a lawyer called Sir Lionel Luckhoo, who made it into the Guinness Book of World Records, famous for an incredible 245 consecutive successful defences in murder trials. It seemed that there were few people on the island who didn't know Kyffin. When I told Sir Lionel why I was visiting Barbados he said, "Tell Kyffin I'll give him a call when we are on the ground."

At the airport we were whisked through customs and passport control. Apparently, any guests of Mr Simpson were considered beyond reproach and ushered through immediately. We didn't need to be checked out. I thought this remarkable until I later learned that the previous week his "guest" had been President Ronald Reagan. And that HM Queen Elizabeth II had only just left. That day I felt like the most important person in the world. I had never been so lavished with grace and made to feel so special – and in one of the most lovely places on earth.

When Julie and I arrived at Kyffin's home his wife, Roberta, was waiting for us on the terrace. She reminded me of Sophia Loren: the smile, the eyes; long elegant dress. We were welcomed and in due course gathered, with a few other guests, around the table for a breakfast of flying fish – a famous local delicacy. The company was lovely and the food wonderful. The backdrop to our conversations was a cacophony of insects, birds and monkeys. Huge frogs leaped around underneath the table, but no one batted an eyelid, as if this sort of thing happened every day. I guess it did! Food, festivity and fellowship in the loveliest of settings with the warmest of hosts. It was simply magical.

After relaxing for the remainder of the day, the next day after breakfast we toured the island; from The Crane on the east to Sandy Lane on the west; the plantations towards the north and the fish markets in villages to the south. On the way home we stopped briefly to experience a local open-air meeting with a

Bajan woman ardently preaching the Gospel. Her message was delivered with such passion that had I not already been saved, that night would have been the one to establish my eternal destiny. I almost felt bad not to have responded! A swim on the south coast concluded the most enjoyable of days. And all because my friend John Wright had suggested I take the trouble to go there and share my story. Unbelievable.

In the West Indies a greater percentage of the population attend church than in the UK. I didn't know this at the time, so I expected that perhaps 100 or so people might turn out for the meeting to hear me speak. But numerous entire families began to arrive and in due course around 2,000 people had gathered. Apparently my visit had been announced the previous week, with Kyffin telling everyone I was one of the "most prolific speakers in the UK". In that instant I understood why he was the success he was: he could sell anything to anyone! This concerned me somewhat, as I wanted to live up to the hype. But I gave it my all and was well received. Kyffin remembers my 3-point message and still reminds me of it, thirty years on.

En route to the airport for our Monday morning flight home via Miami, we enjoyed a final breakfast together on another beautiful Caribbean morning. As we boarded the plan we were directed towards First Class. That would have been nice, but clearly the airline staff had made a mistake. "No, we don't fly first class," I said. But we were! Kyffin had surreptitiously upgraded our seats. And we couldn't even say thank you.

My abiding memory of the trip was being made to feel like a million dollars by Kyffin. It's how he makes everyone feel and that weekend it was my turn. Following his great example I have since done my best to value others similarly; to make people feel good, important, valued, needed, special.

How we treat others says a great deal about us. As the saying goes, "Never trust a person who is rude to a waiter." In a business context, really valuing people – and communicating that to them effectively, not just thinking it in your head – inspires loyalty. It motivates people. It helps them to excel and achieve their potential. Valuing others sounds like such a simple thing to do, yet so few do it. Yet its results are profound and far-reaching. It is another of the building blocks of success.

MARTY THARP – WALKING IN FAITH

One night, around 1980, Julie came home enthusing about an American family called the Tharps who had unexpectedly turned up at our church convention. They were an unusual and talented bunch of people; itinerant preachers and musicians. Marty Tharp looked exactly like Kenny Rogers and sang and played the bass, which contributed to the illusion. His wife Sharon sang as well and played keys.

Over the years Marty became one of my closest friends and another important mentor. He has been a trusted confidante and spiritual advisor. Our relationship began to grow when the family came to stay with Julie and I for inordinately extended periods. They travelled and ministered wherever they were in demand, but sojourned with us for weeks at a time when they weren't. Indeed, it felt at times as though we were living with them and not the other way around. But we didn't mind. We loved having them around and they were always so encouraging.

In order to go far and wide, especially in the USA, the Tharps travelled in a magnificent silver and blue Eagle bus that had been converted into a motorhome. Marty was forever working on it, fixing one niggle or another, but he never complained about it. In later years, our own family would be privileged to travel across a number of states as their guests, ministering alongside them in church services and revival meetings. They were always warmly received and, as a result, so were we.

During one such journey we were travelling at the regulatory 85mph on the interstate, following a large car which was towing a correspondingly substantial caravan, or trailer as they're known in the US. I was standing in the foot well of the bus, beside the door, chatting to Marty as he drove. As we talked I noticed the car's trailer twitch slightly and then begin to swing gently from side to side. The weaving increased, pendulum-like. Instead of being brought under control, it got steadily worse and quickly reached the point of no return, suddenly overturning.

Marty stood on the brakes. The car, dragging the overturned trailer was slowing rapidly, but the 22-tonne bus was not slowing anything like as quickly. I stood transfixed and watched a disaster unfolding. We were in huge danger. In order to prevent us from ploughing into the car and surely killing the hapless older couple inside, Marty yanked the steering wheel, first right, then left. We avoided the car with as perfect a manoeuvre as any F1 driver could perform. But then the weight of the bus and its momentum came into play. With one half of the vehicle on the road, and the other narrowly missing the trees on the grass verge, we hurtled past what remained of the trailer. The grass verge was on an incline, so the bus leaned precariously and cupboards flew open, spilling their contents. It took a full 200 yards for us to pull up. I jumped out of the bus first, followed by my son, Russ. Russ looked back down the highway, wide eyed, and uttered spontaneous words of gratitude: "Thank the God of Jesus!" He knew that we had been saved from more than we wanted to imagine.

For travelling ministry in the UK Marty located and bought

an old coach. It cost a grand total of £350. He re-sprayed it with aerosols! As you walked around the bus it actually changed colour. Over the years this vehicle was replaced by a succession of others that appeared periodically at our home.

Marty enjoyed cars too and before leaving for home one year my brother-in-law, Trevor, gave him his 1970 Daimler Sovereign XJ6. Marty couldn't wait to drive his new pride and joy and since Sharon needed to go shopping in town it seemed like the perfect opportunity. It had been stored in a barn for quite some time, however, and when they set off ten minutes later, a cloud of blue smoke followed them down the road.

While Sharon shopped, Marty spotted a convenient parking bay and pulled up. Having just flown in from the US he was jet lagged and decided to get some shut eye. After a few peaceful minutes he was rudely awoken by a man in a blue uniform knocking on his window and asking what he was doing there. Marty replied politely that he was waiting for his wife. First of all the policeman pointed out the double yellow lines he was sitting on in the "parking bay". Then he noticed the tax disc that had expired five years previously. Marty then assured the officer in his broad American accent that he would get the car MOT'd as soon as practically possible. Oh, and he would sort out some insurance too. The policeman couldn't believe what he had uncovered – a Kenny Rogers impersonator fast asleep on double yellow lines in a completely illegal vehicle! The officer issued the necessary tickets to bring him to justice.

When Marty arrived back at our house he told me all that had happened. I despaired. It didn't look good. Marty, however, appeared unconcerned. He'd been hauled up before the authorities before. What were they going to do? They couldn't send him to jail, after all, he was an American! Rather than sorting the problem out, Marty simply parked up the car, forgot about it and got on with fixing his bus. In due course he simply boarded a flight home to Atlanta, leaving the badly painted monstrosity in our yard.

Some time later, on New Year's Day of all times, the family were all still in bed when the police banged on our front door. They were looking for Marty. Russ answered and told them he wasn't around, he'd gone back to America. I hastily threw on some clothes and went downstairs.

"Does Marty Tharp live here?" a constable asked. "What's all this about him going to America?"

I pointed at the bus. "He lives in that when he's here," I said.

The officer nodded knowingly, "Oh, he's one of 'those'. That's rather the end of this one then, isn't it?"

I agreed and that was the end of the incident.

For all his idiosyncrasies, as others might view them, the Marty I know is a committed, passionate man of faith. Although his lifestyle was, and is, very unconventional, through it he taught me a great lesson. Marty was resourceful and could think out of the box. But the foundation for his life was a sure and certain faith. The bottom line for Marty was an unwavering trust in God. In many ways he modelled good entrepreneurship – a central, unflinching belief in a goal, coupled with the ability to improvise and adapt as necessary. Marty also taught me the value of living for a cause that is greater than ourselves – an issue I addressed at the beginning of this book.

We can learn so much from others if we are prepared to humble ourselves and pay attention. My life mentors taught me how to be entrepreneurial, to work hard and pursue excellence, to value people and to walk in faith. Another mentor taught me the value of having a generous spirit. But that subject deserves a whole chapter of its own (and I'm saving it until last!)

7
THE IMPORTANCE OF CHARACTER

"Integrity is a powerful force,
keeping you alive to others long after you've left their presence."
– MOLLIE MARTI

People often ask me to give them business advice. Frequently, I suspect they are looking for me to impart the "secrets" that will fast-track them towards success with the minimum of hard work and effort on their part. But I don't believe in quick fixes. Over the years I have come to believe that the character of a person is a far more important component in the formula for business success. In fact, it is by far the most important component of the mix in any context in life.

- Motivation is more important than marketing
- Perseverance is more important than PR
- Faith is more important than finance
- Character is more important than commercial ability or cash flow

Every entrepreneur, regardless of their level, faces essentially the same challenges: being forced to think on your feet; trusting your gut feeling often; accepting that with big gains come big losses; remaining agile and being able to adapt to new circumstances; making mistakes, quickly learning from them and moving on ... the list goes on. What will sustain you through all of this and more is character.

SIMPLE WISDOM

When my younger son, Russ, was a little boy, he was renowned for delivering statements that were both dry and astute. He was just 4 years old when we acquired and moved into Ash Tree Farm. Even back then, he was master of the one-liner. Russ and his older sibling, Sam, had visited nearby Clay Hall Farm countless times and watched the tractors busy at work on the land. So it produced a great deal of excitement in both boys when they were informed that we too now owned a farm. They couldn't wait to get there.

When we arrived, however, and I lifted Russ out of his car seat, he looked bemused. Quickly surveying the landscape around him he turned to me with a query:

"Is this our farm, Dad?"

"Yes," I replied.

"Then where's the mud?" he wanted to know.

As far as he was concerned it was mud that made a farm – like Clay Hall – and this one didn't have any – just fields.

This made me smile, but on several other occasions Russ's one-liners have given me significant pause for thought and helped to centre my thinking.

In the early years it was my job, each Monday, to take the boys to Town Close School where they boarded. One particularly wintry morning we were struggling to get out of the drive. The main road was solid with hard-packed snow. We needed a bit of a run up to get through the gate and onto it, even in our 4-Wheel Drive Subaru. Eventually we gained traction and were off, proceeding with caution. The same could not be said for the idiot in a big car who, seconds later, came tearing down the hill in pursuit of us.

Seeing he was driving dangerously fast I determined to slow him down a bit. I slowed my speed and drifted towards the middle of the road. I could see him gesticulating rudely in my rear view mirror, but not willing to back down I touched my brakes. The next thing I knew was an almighty bang as he ploughed into the back of us. I checked the boys were okay and seeing that they were fine, jumped out of the car to survey the damage.

The front of the other man's car was practically demolished; steam gushing everywhere. The Subaru had faired considerably better. I felt justified. "Well, you won't do that again in a hurry, will you mate?" I said, smug that I had taught him a lesson.

After the obligatory exchange of insurance details we were on the road once more. But then Russ pulled his thumb out of his mouth and observed dryly, "I don't think you should do that again, Dad."

Immediately the guilt of my stubbornness caught up with me. Of course, he was right. It was a lesson in character. It's not up to us to punish other people for their irresponsible behaviour. It is our responsibility to moderate our own!

It gave me further pause for thought: others observe the way we behave, and our character is displayed by our actions. What kind of role model are we to those around us? What kind of role model do we aspire to be?

Lesson No.1*: character means we behave consistently and maintain our integrity, even when those around us are behaving badly.*

THE WIN/WIN

I remember the time when I was endeavouring to close a deal to let out our offices to a well known local building society. We were close to finalising the legal paperwork when, at the eleventh hour, the other party's solicitor tried to extract some further benefit from us that had not previously been discussed or agreed.

Later I was chatting to my friend and mentor Bob Gordon about this lack of integrity, undoubtedly letting off steam about it. Russ was home from school and eavesdropping nearby, sitting on the wide window sill in the dining room. Eventually he piped up: "Can I say something, Dad?"

Bob and I turned to look at the 8-year old.

"What I say, Dad," he continued, "is a deal's a deal. That's what I say!"

It was a piece of wisdom that has stood him in good stead throughout his life. And me too.

There is a danger inherent in negotiating deals. It is possible for a business agreement to end up favouring one or other party too much. There is a saying: a deal is only a good deal if it is good for both parties. If a deal is struck that is not a "good deal" then before long someone will become unhappy and want to change it. If a deal is essentially unfair, by being weighted too much in one side's favour, then it won't stand the test of time and short-termism is not good business.

It sounds like a cliché because it is an overused expression, but that's why we must always act with integrity and fairness when making deals and look for the win/win solution, even if that is more inconvenient to us.

You have already read about how I made one of the biggest losses of my career and was defrauded out of a great deal of money. During the court proceedings I found myself in the

High Court being cross examined by a leading QC. In order to defend his frankly defenceless client, he sought to paint me as the more dominant character – i.e. as a ruthless businessman. The conversation went something like this:

"Mr Dacre, you are a businessman?"

"Yes."

"You came to Norfolk with nothing?"

"Yes."

"You are clearly an intelligent man. You have been successful?"

"In some areas…"

"Well, you have made a lot of money. You sold your company for millions. Not bad, eh? Mr Dacre, in business there are winners and then there are losers. Is that not a true statement? I mean someone has to win…"

By implication this man was suggesting that in business, ergo, someone always has to lose. I don't believe that. It's never how I've wanted to do business. It lacks integrity and any business approach that lacks integrity lacks longevity. It can't last. Instead, I have spent my life seeking to ensure win/win outcomes.

Another lesson early on in my career underlined the importance of win/win:

At one point I was the President of the Norwich Chapter of the Full Gospel Businessmen's Fellowship International. For those unfamiliar with the concept, it is similar to Rotary International, but with the added dimension of the message of the Christian Gospel, along with good works. FGB, as it became known, was introduced in Norwich in 1976 by one of the most unique evangelists ever: John F. Wright.

John is an incredible man who remains a great friend and a brother. I have no doubt that when, in time, John arrives in Heaven, in no time he will have re-orchestrated everything such that thereafter they will wonder how they ever managed without him! John was the one who, at FGB dinners, would always be offering to assist someone resolve his company's difficulties. He was an irrepressible character who maintained his verve and enthusiasm regardless of whatever life threw at him. John loved driving – and driving fast. I used to pull his leg about the fact that he was so well known across Norfolk. He enjoyed overtaking other cars and did so at every opportunity. In return he was constantly greeted by the flashing of headlights and waving of arms of other motorists, some presumably happier than others. But that was John – a man in a hurry.

Way back in the 70s we were selling new Opel Kadetts and John had agreed to test drive one. I wanted to sell him one and I remember struggling for the right words as I tried to extol its virtues. The best word I could come up with to describe the Kadett was "wholesome". We both laughed. Eventually John agreed to buy the car for his wife Susan, but only if we could agree a discounted price and part exchange deal.

We then proceeded to haggle for what seemed like hours. After some time we reached the point where we were only £50 apart. But neither of us would back down. We both wanted to have the upper hand and the deal stalled.

The following morning, however, John unexpectedly called me first thing. He told me he had woken up recalling the Bible verse that says,

"A generous person will prosper; whoever refreshes others will be refreshed." (Proverbs 11:25)

In other words, those who act generously towards others will receive generosity in return. What you sow, you reap. John apologised for being mean and told me he would gladly pay the extra £50 for the car. He then told me he'd decided against the part exchange and asked if I would be kind enough to get the new Kadett valeted for him, ready to pick up. Later that day, the car was duly valeted and the deal was done.

Some time later the phone rang. It was John. They had decided to sell Susan's car by advertising it in the local paper. Would I mind housing the car for them at our showroom in order to keep it "nice" and for ease of viewing by potential buyers? Of course, no problem. Shortly after, the phone rang again. It was John. A man had been in touch about the car and wanted to see it. Would I mind showing him round the car as John couldn't make. I agreed to do it. I took this "customer" on the 10-mile road test he insisted on and, in due course, closed the sale. In return for "refreshing" me with an extra 50 quid, John and Sue received £400 more than the offered part exchange price and I did all the work for them! I laughed. If only I had not been so tough in the first place. Win/win is the only way forward. We need to be wise and learn when to stop pushing.

Lesson No.2*: character means we will always seek to be fair and equitable; always look to conduct our affairs with integrity. Ruthlessness is the antithesis of integrity.*

REPUTATION

Being put on the stand and scrutinised by a lawyer caused me to reflect a great deal on the matter of reputation. Over the years I have carried a number of labels. Ones which others used to try and "quantify" me, rather than being self-imposed. I was known as a car salesman. Then a used car dealer. Then a property developer (first as a mystery man; a novice; later as a successful developer). Then I was known simply as an entrepreneur. Then a very successful new car dealer; the owner of the largest car retail business in East Anglia. Then people called me a multi-millionaire. Then a Christian philanthropist.

The fact is, if you become successful, it is like sticking your head above the parapet. You open yourself up to all kinds of suspicion, abuse and jealousy, as well as admiration and encouragement. People will want to label you and try to deconstruct the factors that helped you to get to where you are. I don't really mind what labels people want to stick on me, but there is one tag that I refuse to carry: that of being called a ruthless businessman.

Those who level this accusation seek to justify it: "It's obvious. You couldn't have achieved all you have without being ruthless."

It doesn't occur to them that there is a better path to success: good character and integrity. Doing what we promise to do and doing it well. Keeping our word, even when it hurts us to do so, because "a deal's a deal". Over the years I have sought to go about all I've done – in life, not just in business – according to the following principles. I believe you won't go far wrong if you do the same:

- Put the effort in and work both hard and long
- Pursue the opportunities that come your way and don't give up easily
- Always negotiate fair and square
- Play to your strengths
- Stand your ground when it's the right thing to do
- Seek the wisdom of others and be shrewd and discrete
- Seek to be well informed and make intelligent decisions
- Prepare in advance and think things through well before acting

Ruthless people have no hesitation about riding roughshod over others. They are unconcerned about using others in order to get what they want. They generally exploit those who are weak or vulnerable. They are generally self-interested and self-centred. They are rarely generous. They talk too much about themselves. They find it difficult to be truthful. They are not nice to be around.

I'm reminded of the time when a builder came to Drayton Hall to set out the foundations for a small house we wanted to build in the grounds. It was a Saturday morning and he was working alone. My friend, Ivan Reeve, who was there at the time went over to the man and tried to strike up a conversation.

"What are you doing today?"

"Building a house," he replied flatly. Thereafter the conversation was a little stilted. Then the man said to Ivan, "This place belongs to Graham Dacre, doesn't it?"

"Yes," Ivan replied. "Do you know him?"

"No," he replied, then added, "Don't like the man myself…"

There is not much one can do in such circumstances. Even though he didn't know me, here was a man who had formed a strong opinion about me. He assumed I was a ruthless businessman and I had no opportunity to persuade him otherwise. Canon Andrew White, known as the Vicar of Baghdad and involved in international reconciliation, says, "My enemy is a friend whose story I have not heard yet." So often we make assumptions and judge others without having access to all the facts.

Being unjustly accused bothers a great many people. As a Christian I am grateful for the promise of the Bible that says God will take responsibility for the issue of justice in my life. Whilst some might find this strange or difficult to understand, I find great liberty in leaving my reputation in God's hands. All I need to worry about is obeying Him and keeping my integrity in tact. Here are the words of Isaiah 54:17:

"No weapon that is formed against you will prosper,
And every tongue that rises against you in judgement you shall condemn.
This is the heritage of the servants of the Lord,
And their righteousness is from Me says the Lord."
(Isaiah 54:17 NKJV)

Then there is the promise of God's help from Psalm 18:6:

"In my distress I called upon the Lord,
And cried out to my God;
He heard my voice from His temple,
And my cry came before Him, even to His ears."

Whilst we must seek to live with integrity and treat others fairly and honestly, we mustn't get bogged down in taking ourselves too seriously. We need to hold our reputation lightly. In the end, there is little we can do to change those whose minds are already made up.

Lesson No.3*: character means that we don't waste time trying to justify our actions. Rather, we focus on acting justly.*

PERSEVERING WITH CHARACTER

Some years ago, as one of the trustees of a church, I found myself struggling with the conduct and consideration of the leadership. It was a testing time. Such difficulties in life have a way of bringing our character under the spotlight. How we respond to difficulty, challenges or failure reveals much more about who we are than success does.

I believe that leaders should model exemplary character and

attitude. Others look to a leader and take their cues from them. Leaders therefore have a critical role to play in establishing the culture of any organisation. They model behaviour like a parent models it to their children.

I sat in my office at Norvic House, mentally contending with the conduct and standards of others. I began to pray about it, wanting Him to do something about these "others". He answered my prayer. But not in the way I was expecting. Rather than call others to account, He called me to raise my game. To live to a higher standard; to become a better role model. It was a revelation; a turning point.

I had to agree with God that I was no longer prepared to live according to the lowest common denominator when it came to standards of integrity and character. I was up for raising my game. I was keen to stop criticising others and to allow God to inspect my character instead. Instead of reviewing how others lived, I needed to review how I lived.

I wanted to be more like Jesus and live closer to God. I wanted to know a greater sense of His presence. I was ready to do whatever it cost to get there. The need for two things occurred to me: desperation and determination. It was a turning point in my walk of faith. I had been bruised and discouraged by the behaviour of others. I felt like I had been a lone voice in the desert. But now it was time to climb the mountain and focus only on the presence of God.

Someone once said that we don't increase the brightness of our light by extinguishing someone else's lamp. Too often we seek to prove ourselves right by proving someone else wrong. Comparison is a trap. In the end there is only you and God. That day I learned that we cannot be responsible for the actions of others – only for our own actions – and we must persevere in doing good, regardless of how other people live.

Lesson No.4: *The singer Bono once commented that the success of U2 came about by "a long obedience in the same direction". In the same way, character is produced by perseverance. We don't go with the flow. Rather we learn to keep on living to a higher standard and keep on doing what we know to be right.*

AVOIDING THE TRAP OF COMPARISON

One final thought before we move on. There is great freedom to be found in simply being yourself and accepting who you are, with all of your gifts and skills, flaws and inabilities.

When I first arrived in Norfolk I had no idea of the adventure that lay ahead of me or the great excitement that life would provide. Looking back, I see that at that time I didn't really know what I wanted out of life at all. I didn't really know what I aspired to. Personal expectation was not something I had been taught. Remarkably, self-worth was not something I had been taught to establish either! As a result my self-confidence as a person was almost non-existent. Today I can joke about having asked God to "take away my inferiority complex" and I know plenty of people who would argue that He did a very good job!

The fact is, I struggled with feelings of inferiority until my mid-thirties. Around that time I was trying to expand my business horizons and, alongside being a motor trader, was seeking to become a competent and professional property developer. Viewed from a distance, the people I knew who developed property for a living appeared to have it all together – the lovely wife, 2.4 beautiful children, more than sufficient income and a bright future. This did little to counter my feelings of insecurity and the gnawing doubt that I might be a fraud. If we were scoring people out of 10, such successful entrepreneurs seemed to be 9 out of 10s in every area of their lives. I was certain that I was a 2 out of 10 and therefore had a huge gap to fill that I felt I needed to blag and bluff to overcome.

Eventually, however, after spending some time on the "inside" of this new world, I came to realise that all was not as it appeared to the casual observer. There were certainly areas in which some people were outstanding and showed great competence. But in other areas there was lack, disappointment, heartache and sadness. I decided that in some areas, people were only scoring 4 or 5 out of ten. In more difficult areas, maybe only a two.

I pondered this more and listed the various areas of my life – as an individual, a husband, a father, a friend, a businessman, a member of my local community, a Christian, a bloke… In the end I saw that in some areas I definitely merited a much higher score than I had previously thought. There were areas I needed to work on, but on the whole I came to realise that, on average, I was no worse than anyone else and as good as most.

But the greatest lesson I learned from all this is: we mustn't allow ourselves to fall into the trap of comparison in the first place! I have also adopted a more realistic view of the lives and situation of others and, in so doing, stopped putting myself down.

Today I am grateful to God for the abilities, knowledge and understanding He has given me. My uniqueness is what He has determined for my life and it's what makes me special to Him. Who am I to question what He created, loves and longs to have a relationship with? I no longer feel inferior and I don't put myself down. I continue to work on my "2s", safe in the knowledge that one day Jesus has promised to present me faultless before the Father in heaven.

Lesson No.5: *Accept who you are; who God made you to be. Be realistic about your strengths and weaknesses. Many great entrepreneurs have succeeded because they recognised what they could do and what they couldn't do. To plug the "incapability" gap in their lives they surrounded themselves with good people who possessed complementary skills. But the main thing is that they have accepted who they are and played to their strengths.*

8
THE IMPORTANCE OF THANKFULNESS

"Be thankful for what you have; you'll end up having more. If you concentrate on what you don't have, you will never, ever have enough."

– **OPRAH WINFREY**

An essential ingredient of the character set of the entrepreneur? Without a doubt, thankfulness. *Thankfulness*? Yes. I believe that having a thankful heart, a grateful spirit and an appreciative attitude are vital. Let me explain why as, once again, we think about character, rather than sterile business techniques. In essence...

- Thankfulness means being happy with what we have
- Gratefulness means truly valuing what we have
- An appreciative attitude means acknowledging the source of our blessings by saying thank you, often

THANKFULNESS – THE MISSING INGREDIENT

Some time ago I was asked to give a presentation to a group of business people about what I felt characterised an entrepreneur. I touched on the following points:

- An entrepreneur is generally a person who is likely to be virtually unemployable in any other situation.
- An entrepreneur has aspirations to become financially successful/independent.
- An entrepreneur desires to come up with something new, the next big thing, in order to make their mark.
- An entrepreneur is someone who is up for a challenge, willing to risk all to achieve their ambition.
- An entrepreneur is a leader in the making. They see others succeed and want to emulate that success, though usually on their own terms.

I believe all the attributes above to be accurate and most, if not all, entrepreneurs would admit, "Yes, I see myself here." But listing these points gave me pause for thought. There are other bullet points I could have added that are equally true, such as: an entrepreneur is usually a restless person; unsatisfied; hungry for more; generally over-optimistic. And most want to become millionaires overnight! These are qualities I believe are equally true of most entrepreneurs. But how helpful are they?

I believe in the value of being different and standing out; of aspiring to be financially independent; of being innovative; of being ambitious and taking calculated risks; of desiring success for the right reasons and learning from those who have achieved it.

I don't, however, believe in dissatisfaction and restlessness being the sole motivators for success. I don't believe in always wanting more. I don't believe in making a quick buck.

Thankfulness is the missing "ingredient" from my original list. Thankfulness means being happy with what we have. When we live constantly mindful of all we have to be thankful for, it brings us an inner peace. When we stop to pause, it is amazing just how much we do have to be thankful for – it's just that people so rarely stop to consider.

Why is peace important?

Firstly, because the sense of peace that thankfulness produces helps us to enjoy what we've achieved and what we have as a result of that success. Often, the wealthiest people I've met have not possessed happiness or peace commensurate to their wealth. Far from it. Some of the richest have been some of the most restless and dissatisfied. Wealth has not brought them happiness. Those who think that once they achieve "A" they will happy are misguided. It might bring them peace for a while, but then they will desire "B" and that will become their goal, and so on. "A" was never the problem. A lack of thankfulness leading to a sense of peace was the problem.

Secondly, thankfulness stops us from pushing for things for the sake of pushing, just because we are restless or dissatisfied. Over the years, many companies have come to grief simply because they were determined to grow for growth's sake, instead of being thankful for what they were and what they had already achieved. Growth does not necessarily equal success. Success is doing what you do well and being thankful when positive results come from it. Growth should be a by-product of this, not an aim in itself. As a friend of mine says, "All healthy things grow." And they grow without us trying to force them. Thankfulness is a great tempering agent to counteract our impulsive restlessness.

Similarly, gratefulness means that we are not driven by greed.

Possessing a sense of gratefulness means that we truly value what we have. This means two things to us:

Firstly, gratefulness will ensure that we will utilise the resources we do have properly. We will make the most we can out of them. We won't be frivolous or wasteful. We will also get the most out of them. We will appreciate what we have and enjoy it while we have it.

Secondly, gratefulness will act as a tempering agent in our business transactions. Frequently bad deals are motivated by greed. Doing a deal because we want "more", because we desire to grow for growth's sake, or because we are focused only on making a profit – each of these contributes to a faulty basis for making a deal. Bad deals have no longevity in business. As previously stated, a good deal is only a good deal if it is good for both parties. Bad deals are ultimately counterproductive. They invariably result in generating negativity instead of goodwill.

I consider myself to be a deal maker. I never want to walk away from a meeting without having achieved something tangible. But I realise that the only way to continue being a deal maker is by making good deals! I want both what is good for me and the person on the other side of the table. So much so that before any negotiation takes place, I will sit down and think through what it is that the other person wants. If I can purposefully seek to understand their needs and objectives, then I can structure the "good deal" that will benefit us both. If I sense that what the other person wants is unfair, unreasonable or unrealistic, then there is no point in even having a discussion, because a good deal is unlikely to result. The real objective of business is not to be cute or clever, it is to look for the good deal, because good deals invariably come off. Good deals also invariably generate future business.

An appreciative attitude means that we remember to say thank you. We show appreciation for the source of our success or blessings. We value people. We value relationships. We value our God-given ability to do certain things well, which contributes to our success. Appreciation, properly expressed, goes a long way towards cementing relationships. People don't do business with businesses. People do business with people.

I think it is impossible to be appreciative and properly thankful for a relationship – in life or in business – without being transparent. If we are not open and transparent in our dealings, then surely we are not truly invested in the relationship. If we value a relationship then we will be committed to a level of openness, so that the other party knows that what they see is what they get.

In the past I've done deals with people who held their cards close to their chest; who were reluctant to be open about their objectives and what they wanted from a deal. This just makes the discussion unduly difficult. In such situations I decided to remain transparent regardless. To be completely open. It was disarming for the other person when I laid all my cards on the table and held nothing back. I demonstrated the fact that I valued the relationship more than I valued pressing for a deal.

I was in my early 20's when someone told me about God and suggested that He would want a personal relationship with me. You can read the full story in the Epilogue, titled The Prodigal Son. But my thought process on the night I made that decision ran as follows:

- In truth I acknowledge that I'm not as happy as I could be. Nor am I completely satisfied with my life.
- If God does exist, then I would be very happy to know Him.
- If a relationship is what He is looking for, then I am up for it.

- If, at the same time, I can get rid of my sinfulness and the guilt and shame that accompany it, that would be a great relief.
- If, in the end, I discover that God is not real, all I have to lose is my pride.

I jumped off a metaphorical cliff, not really knowing if God existed, only to discover He was everywhere. It was truly amazing. For me, this change resulted in a reordering of my priorities. It meant that suddenly I was living for a bigger purpose than simply making money. Wealth was given purpose and meaning. It gave me a focus for my life. My faith has guided me when I needed direction; strengthened me when I needed sustaining; motivated me when I could have given up. It has also taught me thankfulness, gratitude and appreciation. The principles that the Bible has revealed to me about how to do life and how to allow my personality to be shaped by God have been the basis of my success and have served me well. No one has been able to come up with an alternative lifestyle that appears anything like as attractive or compelling. Unequivocally, with no hesitation whatsoever, without concern or a shred of embarrassment, I can say that finding Christ has been the best deal I've ever done.

CULTIVATING THANKFULNESS

By now you know a fair amount about me and you know that I love cars. Cars have never just been a product I sold, but a personal passion. What better way to work, than by working with something you love.

When I was 34 I acquired my first ever properly serious sports car – a bright red Porsche 911. I took delivery of it one weekend and come Monday morning I was rather more keen than normal to embark on the short drive to work. Maybe today I would take a more round-about scenic route?

After driving for a while and enjoying the characteristic throaty burble of the Porsche's engine, I came nearer to the city and encountered a refuse lorry which was blocking both my path and my sight. I was already travelling quickly, so without pausing to think I indicated, pulled out and passed the truck at speed. Only then did I realise that the truck was obscuring my view of a long line of traffic leading up to the next roundabout! I was stranded and quickly found myself passing cars on the wrong side of the road. When I finally slowed down, none of the drivers in the queue would let me in. They probably thought, "Look at that flash Herbert trying to push his way in. What a cheek!" I remained hopeful, but as I crawled along looking for someone to be kind to me, the drivers delighted in squeezing up to the person in front. There was no way in.

To make matters worse, the snaking line of traffic was approaching a Police Station. In due course I passed it, along with my uncooperative fellow road users. Only I was still on the wrong side of the road. At this point I might have wished to have been driving a nice little, anonymous looking, black Ford or something similar. Anything other than a bright red 911! It was then that a Police car pulled out of the station and spotted me – an equally red-faced Porsche driver. His blue lights came on almost immediately, the traffic miraculously parted like the Red Sea, and I was pulled over onto the hard shoulder.

Having driven around half a mile on the wrong side of the road I realised I was for the high jump. I buzzed my window down. The policeman leant on my door and looked me up and down. "What did you think you were doing, Sir?" he intoned. I began to splutter some kind of defence. "Before you book me officer, let me explain..." I began. He stopped me in my tracks before I could go further. "Who said anything about booking you?" he asked. He went on to simply give me a good ticking off and told me not to do it again. I was totally amazed at him showing me mercy, when he was quite within his rights to give me a ticket and a much harder time. As it was, the only thing I suffered was a few smug smiles from the motorists filing past me. I was extremely grateful.

This is just one small, car-related incident I thought you might enjoy. The point is, there are so many things in life we can be thankful for. But we have to cultivate an attitude of thankfulness. We are not automatically thankful. I have come to understand that thankfulness is just as much a discipline as taking exercise or practising good time management. It may not come naturally to us, but if we do practice, we'll get better at it.

Thankfulness has many other benefits, besides the ones listed above. If we live life with a spirit of thanksgiving we will treat others as we hope they'd treat us. Looking back, one thing I would do differently in life would be to be less judgemental of others. Thankfulness leads to a lack of judgementalism. We realise that to the same degree that we judge others, we too will be judged. The extent to which we forgive others for their mistakes, or for hurting or offending us, we will be forgiven.

Just like my little example of being clearly in the wrong, caught in the act of being wrong, and yet not being punished for it, "not getting what we deserve" makes us thankful!

I realise that I regularly do things wrong.

Therefore, on the basis that I realise my own need for grace and forgiveness, I no longer want to hold a grudge against those who hurt or offend me. Understanding this has brought me into a place of greater personal freedom. Once again, thankfulness leads back to peace.

24 HOURS TO LIVE

One Monday morning I was chatting to a pastor friend of mine and I asked him what topic he had preached on the day before. He had spoken about the two thieves who were crucified either side of Jesus on the cross. One of the men cried out to Him for mercy and Jesus responded by saying, "This day you will be with me in paradise." Then my friend used another example – a parable Jesus told about a man who spent all his efforts filling his barn. All he was interested in was tearing down his old barns to build bigger ones, so he could stockpile his grain and make a fortune selling it some day in the future. Jesus said the man was foolish because that very day his life would be demanded of him. The man was going to die and all his effort was going to be wasted. He'd spent his life focusing on the wrong thing.

The underlying message of these illustrations was plain to me. It's all about "this day" and what we make of it. We all have 24-hours to live. It's called today. We cannot miss living "today" for all its worth, because tomorrow is never guaranteed. The past has gone and the future hasn't happened yet. All we have to work with is today. This is why thankfulness really is the missing ingredient. It helps us to make the most of now. If you are in any way unsure of my logic, ask yourself this question: "What would I do in the next 24 hours if I knew it was my last?" I know that my time would be spent expressing my thanks for all the things I have to be grateful for.

A New Day

This is the beginning of a new day.
God has given me this day to use it as I will.
I can waste it or use it for good,
But what I do today is important,

Because I am exchanging a day of my life for it.
When tomorrow comes this day will be gone forever,
Leaving in its place something I have traded for it.
I want it to be gain and not loss, success and not evil,
In order that I shall not regret the price I have paid for it.
– GMD

9
HAVING FAITH IN DIFFICULT TIMES

"Never be afraid to trust an unknown future to a known God."
– CORRIE TEN BOOM

UP IN THE AIR

Julie started it all off. In the early 90's she received a typically generous gift from her father. Sedley Pimlott was a man who asked very little for himself, but loved giving gifts to his children and grandchildren. I am hard pressed to bring to mind anyone who was more generous. As a mentor he underlined the importance of living generously. Sedley didn't only give gifts, though he certainly did that, he also opened his heart to people and gave generously of his time, seeking to inspire a similar spark of generosity in others.

On this particular occasion Julie received a cheque for an amazing £12,000. At first she kept it quiet, worried that I might want to "invest" it on her behalf. But she had made up her mind. It wasn't for me to mess with her plans. She informed me matter-of-factly that for the next few weeks I would need to feed myself while she embarked on a special mission. I guessed what might be transpiring and I was correct.

Julie swiftly became the first female pilot in East Anglia to possess a helicopter licence. Even more remarkable than that, she had learned to fly the Robinson R22 – the one machine I would never have on my own licence. I was very proud of Julie when Captain Al Gwilt approved her second ticket (most pilots obtain a private rotary licence first followed by a commercial one).

One thing I have always appreciated about Julie is that she never allows any situation (or person) to phase her. She is comfortable and confident in her own skin. You need that kind of calm, measured single-mindedness if you are going to be a pilot.

Julie has the wonderful ability to wisely and accurately weigh up a situation and her perception of people is rarely wrong. She takes the time to consider and hold things before God before saying anything at all. Over the years I've discovered it is pointless trying to get her to talk before this period of inner contemplation is over. Often, after discussing a matter or person she will say, "Hmm..", which signals the start of a time of personal reflection. Later she will raise the subject by saying, "I've been thinking about x … what I think we should do is…". She is rarely wrong.

Over the years I have enjoyed my cars, and later helicopters, but to Julie these things are but practical tools. Things to get us from A to B efficiently. In the early days of our marriage Julie would drive a car that I enjoyed seeing her in, just to please me (as opposed to something she really wanted to drive). Not so these days!

A few years ago, for example, Julie took me along to the local Land Rover dealer. Although I wasn't initially made aware, we laughed later when Julie admitted I was not there to advise, merely to "facilitate". At one point, when I suggested a car with a contrasting interior colour, Julie just looked at me and said with a smile, "This is my car." The matter was not up for discussion. The new car would, once again, be dark grey with black seats. Three years later it would be the same again. And another three years later, same again please!

Knowing my love for personalised number plates, for a number of years Julie tolerated driving around with JUL15 – until she got fed up of blokes saying "Hello Julie!" whenever she got out of the car.

Julie was similarly resolute in applying her mind to becoming a helicopter pilot. So, in due course, we bought a Schweizer 300c from a local property dealer and it served us well. Owning a helicopter may seem an extravagance to some, but in practical terms it provided an extremely efficient method of conducting business over a large geographical area.

At the time, I was spending most of my time handling property development projects. In property there are certain times of the year when little or nothing seems to happen. The middle of the summer is one; mid-December to mid-January is another. This particular Christmas Julie had seven of her girlfriends staying with us, so it seemed to me the ideal time to escape and get to grips with the helicopter myself. I booked Captain Al Gwilt to begin to teach me how to fly the Schweizer. Forty-five challenging flying hours later I too had my private licence.

Still basking in the glow of success and probably seeking a compliment, I turned to the man who had just taught me to fly, as we waited for the aircraft to cool down before shutting off the engine. "So what's the difference between Julie's flying and mine?" I wanted to know.

He grunted. "Well, let's put it this way," he began. "Whenever I think about your flying the word 'agricultural' comes to mind!"

According to my learned instructor, she was the Porsche test driver and I was the farmer with a tractor! I had to agree that Julie was the smoothest and most able of pilots. She was very, very good.

It was not long after this that we established the Lind Automotive Group and I felt we could justify owning a larger aircraft, more suitable for business rather than hobby flying. We bought a well-equipped Bell Jetranger 3. It had the unusual call sign of G-OONS, but I preferred the more business-like G-LIND. Once it was added to my licence we flew it all over the south east. At the time I was a new face in the BMW network and it gave me a much-needed confidence boost, arriving for meetings by helicopter. More importantly it put my competitors on the back foot, as they had no idea how deep my pockets were!

Considering my humble beginnings in the motor trade, looking out of my office window and seeing this beautiful machine sitting there was really unbelievable. I like to think that I don't have a particularly big ego, but I'm not sure anyone who has the use of a helicopter doesn't have a small amount accompanying it.

I particularly enjoyed taking off and landing. It was satisfying using the autopilot and navigational equipment. And it was a joy seeing others enjoying the experience of travelling in style too. Just like the family who are the only ones in their neighbourhood with a private swimming pool, when you have a helicopter you are never short of friends.

Flying is a great thrill and experience, but is never without risk. This is something my associate Les Brown and I found out first hand on one of our very first trips in the glass bubble Schweizer as we returned from visiting a dealership we owned in Ipswich. It was a salutary lesson both in piloting and trusting God in difficult circumstances.

The weather was rather cloudy this day, but all we had to do was find our way to the A140 and follow it back to Norwich. The doors of the Schweizer are removable and it is permissible to fly with or without them. Being rather macho, Les and I had left the doors back in the hanger, opting for the full 360-degree, exposed to the elements experience.

The cloud base was low at less than 1,000 feet, so we would climb the aircraft up to around 800 feet and head north. We hadn't taken the map with us because we knew where we were going. But not having consulted it, we had simply forgotten about the Mendlesham transmitter. For the uninitiated, this is a 1,000ft high TV/radio mast that serves East Anglia. It suddenly loomed out of the cloud cover to one side of us. We had missed it. But hang on, where were the tensile steel cables that held it aloft? I knew we were in danger of getting tangled up in them so I instantly jerked the stick to the left, taking evasive action. At the same time, Les was looking down and watching the brand new (and very expensive) camera equipment he'd brought with him, sliding across the floor, about to exit the aircraft through the gaping hole where the door should have been. Thankfully, we avoided disaster on both counts.

When things go wrong in a helicopter they invariably go wrong very quickly indeed. That's why, ideally, the helicopter pilot will spend a great deal of time planning and preparing prior to any trip. The trouble with me was that I was impulsive. There was never enough time for preparation. This time, as on many other occasions, I was grateful for the grace of God and the benefit of divine oversight and protection. I needed it!

On another occasion the situation was slightly more serious than my near miss with the radio mast. With the benefit of hindsight, it had all the hallmarks of a tragedy in the making. It was early morning when I lifted off from the farm in Attlebridge. I preferred to have company, but on this occasion I was flying alone.

It was a clear day and I didn't expect to have any issues. After taking a long, low, pleasurable run across our meadows I turned south. After a normal climb I engaged the autopilot and set the linked navigation system to fly the aircraft direct to Eastbourne on the south coast. After travelling out over Suffolk I flew across the Thames above the Queen Elizabeth II Bridge at Dartford. It was always spectacular flying over high land before it fell away, as it did coming into Kent. Then it was out of Kent and into Sussex.

The moving map and on-board systems provide the pilot with an e.t.a., just like a car Satnav, so I knew I wasn't far from my destination. Just a quick jaunt over the South Downs and I would be there. But the cloud cover was thickening. As is often the case, cloud cover masks the tops of the hills and on this particular morning flying under the clouds but over the hills became a bit of a challenge.

At this point I could have considered re-routing but, as usual, I had allowed just sufficient time to get to my meeting, so I decided to press on. Seconds later I entered complete cloud cover and experienced a total white out. A split second before this I had been flying at 100 knots per hour towards hills that I needed more height to clear. Now I couldn't see anything. I looked at my instruments and pulled the stick back, aware that if I didn't have enough height and flew into the hills, that would be the end.

If I didn't get out of the clouds I was in serious trouble, so up I went. But then I had no reference point in order to level the aircraft. I glanced anxiously at the instruments and saw that I was in fact descending at a rate of 1,000 feet per minute. I pulled back the stick again and ascended, but once again couldn't level the aircraft because the gyros took several seconds to communicate the change in direction.

It's amazing what goes through your mind in a perilous situation. I recalled the fatal accident of John Kennedy Jr., who had been killed along with other family members during a similar loss of orientation. I had lost control and I knew it. I had seconds to make a decision. I had only one hope – the autopilot and the grace of God.

Without hesitation I engaged it, setting the heading for 180 degrees and took my hands and feet off the controls. In a symbolic gesture of outward resignation, I could think of nothing else to do but fold my arms and wait to see what happened. I was afraid, but certain of one of two outcomes. Either I was in for a catastrophic crash that would almost certainly end my life or this amazing piece of engineering/electronics would fly itself out of harm's way.

There was no big bang or explosion. After what seemed like an eternity, the cloud broke and I saw land ahead. The dog had carried its master to safety! After that day I vowed never again to fly without a fully functioning 3axis autopilot and I never did. After a successful meeting I flew the helicopter back over the hills that could have so easily claimed my life. I was thankful to God. His hand and His favour had been upon me once again. There were things that I had yet to do, things He had spoken to me about doing that were yet to transpire. I believe He spared me for a purpose and I was incredibly grateful.

There was one further occasion where I learned a bit more about fear and trusting God in the face of difficult circumstances.

I had a meeting scheduled on a Monday morning in Peterhead, located at the easternmost point of Scotland. I took off from home the day before and headed for Carlisle, where I could pause to refuel both man and beast. After stopping off, it was a magnificent trip over the Scottish Highlands towards my destination. Rather than flying over, I circumnavigated the mountains like military jets often do, albeit at much lower speed. It was an unbelievably exhilarating experience, flying low through the valleys, but remaining high enough to clear the lowest points. I remember being able to eyeball puzzled looking sheep staring up at me. I also recall surveying the land beneath me and noting that there were no flat areas where a landing could be made in the event of an emergency. Unhelpfully, my mind pictured a white helicopter tumbling helplessly down the side of a mountain, James Bond style. My adrenalin pumped a little harder.

I arrived safely, however, had my meeting and was soon on my way again, leaving Aberdeenshire behind me and heading once again into the majesty of the Highlands. By the time the mountains came into view there were just small pockets of cloud surrounding them, so again I opted to fly zigzags around the hills, seeing if I could make my way through without having to climb higher. As long as there was sunshine ahead I was fine. The clouds appeared to be caught up on the hills. Ahead of me was the bottom of a lovely "V" and I was aiming directly for it. My height was perfect. It was a simple matter of flying just feet above a narrow plateau with rock walls to either side. I was travelling at 100+ knots per hour and it was fantastic. So much fun.

But in an instant, everything changed. As I passed a range of hills, a wall of solid white cloud swept in from the right and wiped out my vision. I knew I had a rock floor only feet below me and a mountain face to my left and right. The V I had been aiming for was completely obscured. Flying directly into a bank of cloud like this was contrary to everything I had been trained to do. This was big time scary. My most immediate concern was drifting to one side or the other and striking the rotor blades on the rock face. Or alternatively, the skids catching the rocks below me and flipping me over.

I was so scared I was literally paralysed by fear. This is hard to explain if you've never personally experienced it, but whilst my mind continued to function, my body refused to comply. The temptation to black out swept over me and I had to resist it with all my might just to remain conscious. I actually slapped myself, hard. Within seconds, thankfully, I emerged from the cloud. Suddenly I could see where I was and, miraculously, I had stayed on course through the V. Now I knew what it meant to be paralysed with fear. It wasn't just a mental condition. I could believe that, in the most extreme of situations, fear could literally claim a life.

Both relieved and exhausted I expressed my thanks to God for, once more, bailing me out and compensating for my somewhat reckless behaviour. It was then that He reminded me of the words of Psalm 139:

"O LORD, You have searched me and known me.
You know my sitting down and my rising up;
You understand my thoughts afar off.
You comprehend my path and my lying down,
And are acquainted with all my ways.
For there is not a word on my tongue,
But behold, O LORD, You know it altogether.
You have hedged me behind and before,
And laid Your hand upon me.
Such knowledge is too wonderful for me;
It is high, I cannot attain it.

Where can I go from Your Spirit?
Or where can I flee from Your presence?

If I ascend into heaven, You are there;
If I make my bed in hell, behold, You are there.
If I take the wings of the morning,
And dwell in the uttermost parts of the sea,
Even there Your hand shall lead me,
And Your right hand shall hold me.
If I say, 'Surely the darkness shall fall on me,'
Even the night shall be light about me;
Indeed, the darkness shall not hide from You,
But the night shines as the day;
The darkness and the light are both alike to You."
(Psalm 139:1-12)

God pointed out to me that He was with me throughout this drama. Even though I was stricken with fear, He was there and remained in control.

I learned several important things from each of these experiences.

First, once we have made the step of consecrating our lives to God, there is nowhere we can go without Him also being there. He is utterly committed and devoted to us, His children, and He has promised never to leave us or forsake us (Hebrews 13:5).

Second, though we may panic when we find ourselves plunged into difficult or dangerous circumstances, God remains constant and faithful. Even when we have manufactured those circumstances ourselves, God doesn't lose patience with us. His grace knows no bounds. An earthly father might get angry at a recalcitrant child and say, "Have it your own way then! You're on your own." But not our Heavenly Father. Instead He remains close by, waiting for us to yell for help so that He can step in and rescue us. He remains constant and faithful, even when we are needlessly or deliberately reckless.

Third, when under pressure it is so easy to turn to human wisdom or logic for answers. We try to think of ways in which we can escape our present predicament and look for this or that solution. Invariably, the best solution is to stand still, take our hands off and relinquish control of the situation to Him. The only thing that will save us from a potentially devastating outcome, whatever the challenge we are facing, is divine wisdom. Frequently God's solutions defy human logic, but they work 100% of the time.

Fourthly, it is in the most testing and difficult times that we learn dependence on Him. Indeed, it is at these times that we are made starkly aware of the depth of our need for dependence. Especially when we have nothing and no one else left to depend on! In this respect, challenging times afford us a blessing because they teach us where our priorities lie. We were made to be dependent on our Maker. Designed to walk and work in cooperation with Him. During difficult times we begin to realise why.

Lastly, the biggest lesson I learned is that the Holy Spirit is our autopilot for life. Left in charge of the controls of our life, metaphorically we soon navigate into cloud cover, get lost and put ourselves in danger. In testing times, returning control to the Autopilot and taking our hands off the situation is a difficult but vital move. We need to learn to be quicker to say, "God, I won't even attempt to handle this situation. You take control." Those who are resourceful and have certain gifts and abilities find this harder to do. Self-reliance militates against faith and trust. But life simply works better when you allow God to be in control of it.

If you want to be successful, there is success in surrender. Rather than a sign of weakness, it is a sign of great strength and character.

10
DEFINING YOUR CULTURE

"We are what we repeatedly do.
Excellence, then, is not an act, but a habit."
– ARISTOTLE

Something that remained a constant source of amazement to me throughout the years of running the Lind group was how much could be achieved from a farm office containing only myself and my excellent personal assistant Carolyn Hucknall. Frequently, simple is better. Why go to the trouble of acquiring and fitting out costly office premises for a business' HQ, when all that is needed is a couple of desks, two phones and some filing cabinets? Much was achieved in our business simply by regular visits to dealership premises in order to build strong relationships with the management teams responsible for running them day to day. Summoning dealership principals to a faceless, soulless corporate headquarters was not how I wanted to operate. It would have communicated the wrong message. Over time, therefore, I realised how important it is for us to determine the culture in which we want to operate. I also realised that organisational culture need not be something that just emerges of its own accord – we can and should define it.

This thinking began to crystallise for me when the principal of one of our newly appointed Audi dealerships phoned me one day. Since he was leading a newly assembled team, he wanted to host an evening for all his staff, to help them to gel together. He asked if I would be willing to come and speak for half an hour on the "culture" of the Lind group.

"Certainly," I responded confidently, "Just let me know the date."

I put the phone down, pencilled the date in my diary and promptly forgot all about it. It was three months away, after all, and I had many more pressing matters to attend to. With the matter filed away, the weeks flew by. Soon the day was approaching and it became necessary for me to give it some thought.

It was then that I realised I had no clue what to say! I didn't really know what culture was and consequently had given no thought to what ours was, what it should be or what value it would contribute to the business. As far as I knew, "culture" was something to do with art. I had been called a "patron of the arts" because I had funded some local initiatives, but to be honest it meant little more to me than bankrolling something that everyone seemed to enjoy except me!

I set about thinking the matter through. I cleared my desk, took a new A4 pad out of the stationery cupboard, pulled a dictionary and thesaurus from the bookshelf and set about unlocking the secrets of the commercial universe. What was culture? How was it described? What did it do? How did it relate to us and our business endeavours? More to the point, what could I possibly say about it?

It proved to be a fascinating and instructive morning. By the end of it I had come to realise that whilst culture is not visible, it can most definitely be seen. In our context, our culture determined the "spirit" that we as a team collectively manifested. Culture was critical! Our culture set the values we took on board and lived by daily. Those values determined our behaviour and actions. And our behaviour and actions dictated whether our customers had a positive or a negative experience with us. In short, our culture had the power to influence our success – or our failure.

I then realised that culture could be predetermined. We didn't have to leave it to chance and hope that what emerged was good. Many organisations do this. They hope that if they hire enough good people, then a good business culture will result. I think this is putting the equation back to front. It is certainly possible to have a group of good people all doing the wrong thing! On the contrary, if we firmly establish the values by which we want to live and operate up front, then focus on helping every person to take them on board, good people will find an environment in which they can flourish. And even "less good" people will be given something to aspire to!

I also realised that as the leader of the Lind group, it fell to me not only to specify our culture but also establish it by being the first to model it. I had to champion our cultural values. I had to be able to convey the desired culture to others with passion, so that they too would be willing to embrace it. Suddenly culture was at the top of my list of priorities. I could already see that creating a good one would prove to be immensely valuable.

DETERMINING YOUR CULTURE

Over the ensuing weeks and months I defined and distilled to its essential ingredients what I wanted the Lind group culture to look like. We eventually developed this into a booklet that we provided to every single member of the organisation, regardless of their role. It proved to be a huge asset. It provided a point of reference; a filter through which everyone could consider how they conducted themselves in the business. Over time the values I championed became engrained throughout the group. We had established a culture.

In your context, whatever job you do or whatever aspect of business you are involved in, you may like to ask yourself the following questions:

- What is the current culture of my organisation?
- What values does our culture reflect?
- Am I satisfied with that culture?
- What are the benefits of having a first class culture?
- How do I go about raising the standard of our culture?
- If the culture is not all I would hope for, how do I go about changing it?
- How can I motivate others to aspire to a more vibrant, successful culture?

Only you can answer these questions in your context. But the answer to the last three questions, which refer to culture change, is simple: you are the answer! Culture change begins with individuals. If you want your culture to change then you have to become a role model for the new culture you want to build, and consistently model it to others.

After much thought, we mapped out the following cultural values for the Lind group. I summarise them here in the hope that they will provide a useful point of reference for your own deliberations.

What is culture? A set of values and principles that set standards and determine ethos.

What is a business culture? A successful business culture reflects the ideas, attitudes, customs and values shared by a committed team of professionals working together for a common purpose and gain.

What are the benefits of a culture? 1) Like the unseen keel of a ship which maintains a vessel's stability, a strong culture provides a firm foundation for an organisation. 2) A vibrant corporate culture generates a great company performance. A weak culture will produce indifferent results. 3) A defined culture provides a framework for working. It generates a sense of identity, security and purpose and provides feelings of belonging, inclusivity and exclusivity.

What are the characteristics of our culture: The following are our intrinsic values:

- Excellence
- Integrity
- Professionalism
- Honesty
- Innovation
- Focus

We impressed on ourselves the need to constantly ask, "How should I act in this situation in order to best reflect Lind values?" In addition we developed a saying that we repeated like a mantra: Do it. Do it right. Do it now.

In our booklet, we expanded on each of the six core values above, so that members of the organisation could easily see how each could be practically applied to their work. Take "integrity" for instance.

Integrity means that...

- In all we do we must be honest
- In all we say we must be truthful
- In financial dealings we must be fair and reasonable
- We must apply best industry practices in each and every department
- We must not overcharge for products or services
- We must always honour our commitments, undertakings and warranties
- We must always do what we say we'll do

In a nutshell, integrity is doing the right thing, even if no one is watching.

I placed "excellence" at the top of our list of six values. It belongs there because I believe that cultivating a spirit of excellence is paramount. If excellence runs through everything we do, then the other values will naturally fall into place. Striving for excellence at every level is a critical factor in the success or otherwise of any business or service.

CULTIVATING A SPIRIT OF EXCELLENCE

What is excellence? It is the state of excelling. To be excellent something has to possess outstanding merit and quality. It is naturally superior; comfortably preeminent. When we excel, we surpass previous performance. Excellence need not be accompanied by arrogance and pride, but can exude a quiet confidence in hitting the mark every time. Excellence produces a consistently great performance. It means being top class and staying there.

After working hard to establish excellence as a value at every level of the business, I never tired of hearing our customers' feedback: "Your staff are wonderful … your after-sales service team are quite exceptional … they are truly first class." And it was true! Did we always get it right? No. But we got it right so many times that we built up a huge amount of "credit" with our customers. So much so that when we recognised our mistakes and apologised they instantly forgave us.

Excellence had been something of a personal mission for me. Looking back, it wasn't a value that was on my radar when I was growing up. My parents were good, upright, hard working people, of course, and both sought to do things well, but excellence wasn't part of our world, our culture or our conversation.

Throughout my 20's I sold used cars. I worked hard and sold a car to everyone I could talk into buying one. I became comfortable in this environment and I excelled at it. But when, in the 1980's, I turned my attention to the property sector, I found a far higher level of commercial professionalism, competence and integrity. I immediately knew I had to raise my game if I was to find acceptance among the professionals within the city. To be completely honest, I realised that some of my practices were not as good as they should be. I felt I needed to challenge the standards that I was living and operating by. I needed to come to a very clear sense of...

- What was right and wrong (integrity)
- The standards to which I would aspire (excellence)
- What needed to change in me if I was live according to these higher values

First, I took an honest inventory of where I had failed in the past and determined how I wanted to live in the future. I endeavoured to put right any situations that had been left unresolved. Secondly, I looked at the areas in which I could improve:

- I determined to be more straightforward in all my dealings
- I learned to listen to, and respect, the opinions of others
- I sought, and had regard for, professional advice
- I began to associate with those who were intellectually brighter than me and learned from them
- I upgraded the professionalism of my working environment
- I reduced the number of words I spoke by half and made the ones I used count for twice as much!
- I refused to allow the standards of others to determine the standards I set for myself

I remember on one occasion another car dealer telling me, "I'm fed up with customers, they always tell lies! They come and tell me they've been offered £7,000 for their car, when I know full well it's only worth £6,000 and no dealer would have offered them £7,000."

I challenged him: "What would you do if you were negotiating to buy a car? Would you say it was worth £7K or £6K?" He admitted that he'd probably say it was worth more than it really was. The point was made. We have to consider those things we do not appreciate in others and make sure that we don't do them ourselves!

All of this was incredibly valuable, but excellence is relative. Later, when I had the opportunity to become a BMW dealer I quickly came to appreciate just how professional they were. My involvement was going to require another quantum leap and a further upgrade of my standards. To this day I have the highest regard for BMW's professionalism and intelligence. I learned a great deal about establishing strong brand values and understood more about the connection between culture and brand success. I sought to raise my game and embrace the BMW culture of excellence. I took the best of BMW and overlaid it with the principles for success that I found in the Bible. The results were amazing. When we began, the BMW dealership in Norwich was regarded as one of their weakest performers. Over the years that the dealership was run by the Lind team it became one of the most respected centres in the whole of the UK.

UNLOCKING EXCELLENCE IN OTHERS

I cannot overstate the importance of business leaders being role models for their business culture. The way in which those at the top operate filters down through the organisation and touches every area. My experience is that those who operate at the coal face reflect the spirit that exists behind the closed doors of the boardroom.

If I'm always smiling, my team will smile. If I'm always grumpy, then my team will be miserable. If I'm real with my colleagues, they'll be real when they're interacting with customers. If I tell the truth, my team will generally be truthful too. If I'm honest, they are likely to be honest too. But if I'm a tricky, slippery operator, I'll likely attract similar people to work with me. The key to drawing excellence out of those around us is becoming a champion of excellence ourselves; modelling it effectively and inspiring others to do the same.

A great synergy is created when people work together with like-minded values. Pursuing the goal of excellence as a team means that much of this synergy happens in a natural, unforced way. Every business leader will tell you that it is vital to have good people around you. But good people are not good enough unless there is a common culture aimed towards a common purpose.

I fondly recall many members of the Lind group who were similarly committed to excellence. Sue Curtis was one who came to reflect the spirit of Lind perhaps more than anyone else. As a result she became one of my most loved, valued and trusted employees. Long before we met Sue was already one of the longest serving people in the entire BMW network. Everyone loved her. She was like a mother to many, but at the same time not someone to mess with. To celebrate one of her landmark achievements in the company I once took her out for an afternoon's flying in one of my helicopters.

Colin Jacobs was a character I inherited when we acquired BMW Norwich. He too was well known throughout the network. In his office, his multiple achievements were plastered all over the wall. He had relocated from London to run the after-sales department. When things didn't shape up quite as he'd imagined he grew restless. He gave me the impression that he might leave and some weeks later he was offered a job in Cambridge.

Whenever someone was about to leave, I invariably encouraged them to reflect on their decision before finally handing in their resignation. I told Colin that I wanted him to stay and that if he did, he would be here by choice and not because he felt he had no other option. Colin stayed. He became one of my "lifers" – one of those I knew would never move on. Colin raised the standard of excellence in our after-sales service such that he produced a top, national level performance quarter after quarter without ever appearing to work hard.

Brian Hensman has been a lifelong friend and advisor. As a newly qualified rookie accountant he worked on my Grandad's accounts. Later he took over responsibility for my parents' financial affairs. Then he has personally looked after me since I was in my 20s. Brian is intelligent, logical, consistent, honourable and dependable. If only the world had a few more people like him in it.

There are numerous names I could mention; numerous people I could write about. But space doesn't allow. The fact is, though, nothing of any substance can be achieved alone. Very little of value is established without the help of others.

Once I was asked by Harley Davidson to produce my CV. They didn't really need one as such, but the application form to acquire a Harley Davidson franchise requested one, so I found an old one and updated it. Under Education I wrote "Limited". Under Qualifications I wrote "Few". Under "Reasons for your success" I wrote "I didn't know how to stop!" More seriously, if I was pressed to say what has been my most significant achievement in business, I would say it has been having the good sense to surround myself with people much cleverer and more able than me!

KEYS TO CORPORATE SUCCESS

If you were to ask me how to achieve success in your business, I would tell you to establish a culture of excellence with aspirational values. If you want more detail than that, here is a short list of the things we did and the standards we maintained. Once these cultural values were established and lived out, the success of the business took care of itself.

- We put people first and valued/respected staff and customers alike
- We always did what we said we would do, keeping our promises and honouring our word
- We endeavoured to get things right first time

- We never lied or fudged the truth
- We admitted our mistakes and put matters right, regardless of the cost
- We were passionate, focused and vision-led
- We set high standards for ourselves and others
- We looked the part, talked the part and acted the part
- We anticipated challenges and worked to overcome setbacks
- We kept moving forward, despite any disappointments

In addition, I sought God before making any major decisions. I continued to give out of all I earned and we also tithed out of our company profits, giving 10% away to good causes every year. If you are willing to invest yourself in establishing a great culture for your organisation too, I believe you will see similarly outstanding results.

"Excellence is the result of caring more
than others think is wise, risking more
than others think is safe, dreaming more
than others think is practical, and expecting more
than others think is possible."
–Ronnie Oldham

11
THE IMPORTANCE OF FAMILY

"A family is a place where principles are hammered and honed on the anvil of everyday living."
– CHARLES R. SWINDOLL

I have already made mention in this book of the fact that very few "successful" businessmen can become or remain successful without the support of a great team around them. Whilst this is so valuable, however, the love and support of one's family is utterly essential. Family is the place where we can learn by making mistakes and not get kicked out. It is the place where we can retreat from the sometimes bruising battlefield of business. It is also a place that levels us whenever we become intoxicated by our success and begin to take ourselves too seriously. Family knows the best and worst of us – yet still loves us.

MISS JULIE

I was sixteen when my parents upped sticks and moved to

Norwich. I didn't really want to move and found some digs in a small village north of Maidstone. Shortly after my Aunty Eunice offered me a room in her home in Cranbrook. It was a lovely motorcycle ride home each day from the paper mill factory in Aylesford where I had my first job. I challenged myself to see how fast I dare take the long, sweeping bends. Thankfully, I never came to grief in the process.

From there, I can't quite recall how I came to be living in a touring caravan, parked in the front garden of my friend, David Robertson's parents house. I worked shifts and survived on a bowl of cornflakes in the morning and a meal in the evening. I went to the same café for supper every night. My only vice was smoking Guards and a pack of ten would last me two days. My living arrangements were fine during the summer months, but living in an unheated caravan during the winter months was a challenge. One day I tried to open the caravan door to go to work and it refused to budge. Eventually, heaving it open, I saw the snow must have been about eighteen inches deep. After that it was freezing and certainly no fun crawling into a damp bed every night. At least my milk lasted longer!

I went to visit my parents in Norwich. I really hadn't intended it to be anything other than a flying visit, but I was so undernourished and miserable that on completing the 120 mile trip, I arrived home and just collapsed. Mum sorted out my bedroom and insisted I stay. It wasn't too long afterwards that the computer job at Boulton and Paul was advertised and, full of self confidence, I was taken on. Now I had a reason to remain in Norwich – a job and a warm, dry bed on the second floor of 190 St Clements Hill.

I will never forget dismantling my Triumph T500 motorcycle in the garage there. As I refurbished or cleaned each part thoroughly, I stored the bits I'd worked on in my bedroom. It was there that I later reassembled the entire bike. After all that hard work it looked absolutely wonderful. Then I realised I had no way of getting it down the stairs!

At nineteen I had been driving for several years but had only ever passed my bike test. I had lessons with BSM and was quickly ready for my driving test. I passed with flying colours. At the time my dream car was a 2.0 litre Triumph Vitesse. Armed with an "official" driving licence my skills were put to good use in the family and this paved the way for my first tentative steps into the motor trade. My uncle John would sell the bangers he took in part exchange at his growing used car business in Sittingbourne, Kent. Dad would send me over to John's to buy them for £25, whereby I'd drive them back to Norwich. There we would polish them up as well as we could and sell them for between £50 and £75. On one such trip I pulled over to pick up a hitchhiker on the outskirts of Chelmsford. Unfortunately, doing so brought me and my vehicle to the attention of an eagle-eyed local policeman. He immediately stopped me and began to inspect the car. He wasn't impressed with my four, completely bald tyres. Cheekily, I asked him what he expected for £25! He stoically issued me my first ever ticket.

Although I had been somewhat ambivalent to my parents' enthusiasm for church, I unexpectedly enjoyed attending Mount Zion church. There were two full-on services every Sunday. Sunday morning lasted around two hours. The evening service began at 6.30pm and we rarely got out before 10.00pm. Pastor Sedley Pimlott could talk! Looking back, I had a number of delightful girlfriends, but none took my heart like Miss Julie Pimlott. She was beautiful. Slightly younger than me, she was very level headed and worked for her father on his farm. We began dating in the Spring of 1973.

From the beginning I knew that Julie was "the one", and so sought to raise the subject of marriage with Sedley (I chose to do so in Sedley's outside sauna!) Sedley was the most congenial man, but talking to him about something he didn't want to talk about was always a challenge. This was one of those subjects. I nudged, prodded and hinted but got nowhere. The most I could elicit from Sedley was, "You'll need to talk to her mother!" I already knew that would be a waste of time. She had made it crystal clear that she didn't approve of me. She must have had her reasons, but I never knew what they were. It was Margaret Thatcher who once said, "The lady's not for turning." Neither was Mildred. The only difference between Mildred and Margaret was that I've heard it was possible to negotiate with Mrs Thatcher…

Nevertheless, Julie and I wanted to be married and as we began to plan the wedding the reluctance on the part of Mr and Mrs Pimlott began to abate somewhat. We were married on March 29, 1975. Our first home was on St Clements Hill. It was near Friday's Car Sales and not far from Julie's parents at Beulah Farm, Hainford. Julie and I decorated it from top to bottom and remained there for three years.

One of my lasting memories is when, shortly after we were married and I was looking to stamp my authority on the relationship, I said to Julie, "Now look here, Julie. Who's the boss in our marriage?" We were standing in the kitchen. Without hesitation she responded, "In here, I am!" We burst out laughing. I realised immediately that it was a partnership and we were both "the boss" in a number of different areas. It was never an issue after that and has remained that way ever since.

On July 22, 1977, our first son, Samuel Edward was born. Julie was more than ready for him to make his appearance by the time he arrived. Sam's birth was the first time I laid eyes on Drayton Hall. Little did I realise how much it would feature in our lives in years to come. Sam's arrival transformed our house into a home and brought a sense of family. Life would never be the same again.

SAMUEL EDWARD

Sam was a lovely boy. Mentally strong – always very determined – and at times too clever for his own good. I can remember two things about the night he was born. The first was enjoying a late night bowl of cornflakes just before the action began. Cold milk. Sparkling sugar. Wondering whether I would actually like the baby and whether he would like me! The second was Sam's birth itself. The jumbled up feelings of anxiety and euphoria, all mixed together. The realisation that there was no need to worry any more. I loved him from the moment he appeared.

RUSSELL BARCLAY

We were happier still when Russ arrived and our little family expanded. Sadly, this time I wasn't able to witness the birth. Hearing he was about to appear, I dashed over, but Russ landed just before I arrived. Once again we were delighted to welcome him to the family. Russ was a good natured, peaceful boy, in many ways more at ease with the world than Sam. But both were high spirited and we loved them dearly.

AN ANCHOR IN CHALLENGING TIMES

I had never needed to dig deep to find the motivation to work hard, but having two small sons to look after helped. For me, living and working for them was providing for their future. So I worked hard and enjoyed the time I did get to spend with them.

Many people dream of success, but success always has a cost.

Not everyone is prepared to pay it. When I began selling cars for a living, Julie and I lived a matter of minutes away from my work. I could have easily gone home for lunch each day, but I never did. I was always the first to arrive and the last to leave. Then, when I got home, there was still always some deal that I needed to close. Julie was remarkably patient with me.

Whilst I was very good at putting food on the table and providing for the family, I had little time or inclination for anything else. I worked hard six days a week, but never on a Sunday, which was always reserved for church. Apart from that, I saw the boys for a few minutes in the morning and again in the evening. Julie made up for me. She was a natural born mother and is undoubtedly the reason why Sam and Russ have turned out as well as they have. Looking back, I know I should have spent far more time with them. I regret not doing so.

Julie has never been one to complain. For her to admit she is feeling unwell normally means she is quite poorly. It was around 1980 that she first became sick. I could see that she wasn't well, but initially I put it down to her recovering from giving birth to Russ. It soon became evident it was more than that. Things came to a head one night when she woke up bleeding profusely from her mouth. We threw on some clothes and hurried to the local A&E where Julie was immediately placed in an isolation ward.

In due course we found out that her lungs had been damaged by a bout of Tuberculosis. A large part of the lining of both lungs was severely scarred. We were very concerned. Julie less so than me. Her faith in God was strong and she couldn't understand all the fuss. Of course she would recover. Of course she would be alright. Anyone who visited her bedside left encouraged by the words of faith she spoke. After what seemed like an eternity Julie was allowed out of hospital and returned home, but the damage was clear to see. Clearing the lungs required daily exercises and her coughing was painful to hear, let alone endure. I remember that when she coughed it was violent enough to vibrate the front door bell.

An unbidden situation like this punctures our otherwise happy life and can be hard to deal with. We are left with many questions. Why has this happened? What will the future hold? Suddenly life had changed and the way ahead was far less predictable. When we married, we did so for better or worse; richer or poorer; in sickness and in health. It's just that no one ever anticipates being sick.

But over four decades later, here we are. Throughout all these years, despite the health challenges and the ups and downs, Julie has remained my balance; my constant, sure companion. She was a remarkably confident person when I met her and she has remained thus. More remarkable still, since we've been married nothing I've done has ever phased her! She remains faithful, wise and discerning and has the gift of being able to read accurately people and situations. I am a much better person for having married her. I couldn't possibly have been successful in business without her.

A LEVELLER

Family is a great leveller. It helps us remember where we came from and it is the place we always refer back to. Family helps us keep our feet on the ground and stops us taking ourselves too seriously.

When I was growing up, we didn't know any "posh" people as we termed it. There certainly weren't any living on our street. I didn't understand what public schools were – weren't they just where the public goes? Universities? No one in our family had ever contemplated going to one. So it was completely new territory when Julie and I found ourselves in the fortunate position of being able to send our boys to a very good local preparatory school. When I was a kid, no one ever had to worry about school fees. No one was ever behind in paying them. There weren't any to think about! But we wanted to give our boys the best possible education and set them up for the future. It was St Christopher's School to begin with. Then Town Close Prep School, followed by Gresham's School.

Gresham's was a boarding school and each Sunday evening I would drive the boys back after their weekend at home. One evening we were chatting away as we drove. I was seeking to encourage them. I suggested they made the most of their school life. After all, it wouldn't last forever; a blink of the eye and it would be gone. "So enjoy it as much as you can boys," I said.

Sam piped up.

"Why's that Dad?" he asked. "Because you're paying for it?"

I thought of saying, "Listen Sam, that's not the point." But I chose to ask a question instead.

"How much do you think it will cost in school fees over the years anyway?"

"A hundred thousand?" Sam guessed.

"Well let's use that figure, one hundred thousand," I said. Then, trying to be provocative added, "That's one hundred thousand you won't get when I die isn't it? Fifty thousand each. So effectively, your paying for your school fees, not me! That's why you ought to make the most of it."

All went quiet in the car. A few miles down the road Russ spoke up.

"Does that mean we are paying for your cars then Dad?!"

Cheeky monkey. We all laughed.

"The only rock I know that stays steady,
the only institution I know that works is the family."
–Lee Iacocca

12
LIVING GENEROUSLY

"There is no exercise better for the heart than reaching down and lifting people up."
– **JOHN HOLMES**

"You have not lived today until you have done something for someone who can never repay you."
– **JOHN BUNYAN**

Being in the position of having significant funds at your disposal brings with it the responsibility of stewarding those resources effectively. You will notice that I've mentioned this theme several times elsewhere in this book, because I believe that we are all called to live for something bigger than ourselves. Having lots of money can provide a pleasant distraction for quite a while, but in the end it doesn't satisfy the hunger of the soul. Every person on the planet was born to live beyond themselves, not to live consumed by their own selfish needs and desires.

There is great joy to be had in giving. We may give occasional, extravagant gifts to family or our wider circle of friends. We may even indulge in isolated, random acts of generosity to those who don't expect it. But a higher calling than either of these is to live with a spirit of generosity – by which I mean to have the ability to hold all our possessions lightly, so that we are free to touch the lives of others whenever we are moved to do so.

My father-in-law, Sedley, was my role model in this. An incredibly generous man, both with his time and money, he took a genuine delight in giving to others. Fundamentally, he had learned the joy of a generous spirit.

I became aware of Sedley (before I met his daughter), many years ago when we lived in Maidstone. Mum and Dad had met him a number of times at revival meetings and had begun travelling to Norwich occasionally to attend Mount Zion church where he was the Pastor. The revival meetings had birthed a new joy in many people's lives and caused churches like Sedley's to be completely reinvigorated. People were overtaken with a new sense of freedom and their relationship with God was transformed. This attracted the interest of my parents.

So began the start of our family gravitating towards Norwich. When they finally took the decision to move once again – as we'd done so many times as a family – they did so lock, stock and barrel. The sense that God was calling them to be a part of this re-envisioned church was the decisive factor, so they made the move in faith, with no specific jobs to go to. Generating a new source of income was therefore an immediate concern. They had insufficient capital to secure a mortgage, so Dad or Mum, or both, needed a job.

Sedley was a caring pastor and soon demonstrated his

generosity. He loved people – being around them, helping them. He frequently helped us out. He and his sons bred pigs and, in order to feed them, they would collect out-of-date food from fish shops all over Norwich, as well as local factories. Once in a while he would also relieve Birdseye of all their just out-of-date supermarket stock, and did so by the lorry load!

As a result, boxes of burgers, beef in gravy and frozen ready-meals arrived at regular intervals and filled our freezer. Just when we began to worry we would have no food, it was like Christmas had arrived. I'd never seen so much food in one place. It has to be said, we would often have burgers for breakfast, lunch and supper! But this seemed completely normal to us and we never complained. We had been fed through Sedley's generosity and for that we were hugely grateful.

TWO HALF-CROWNS

Whenever Grandad came for a family visit, he would always give each of his grandchildren some money as he said his goodbyes. Most often it was a florin or a half-crown. My parents constantly encouraged me to save these gifts in my Post Office savings account, but I rarely did. On one occasion, however, Grandad gave me two half-crowns. Now this was serious! They were beautiful coins to look at and to have two of them, wow!

The following week our family attended a revival meeting in London to hear the celebrated evangelist A.A. Allen. I remember walking the streets around the Elephant and Castle holding these two oversized coins in my pocket and thinking I could have anything I wanted. I was rich!

Later, at the meeting, I listened to A.A. Allen preaching. He was one of the most compelling communicators of his day. He was speaking about raising funds for a mission in Africa. In my pocket were the two half-crowns, still waiting to be spent. The offering bucket began to pass through the congregation and I had a decision to make. I began to sense that God wanted me to put half of my recently inherited fortune into the offering. But as the appeal continued, I realised it had to be more. Indeed, He wanted me to give everything! And that is what happened to my two half-crowns.

After the service I was just a boy again and a poor one at that! But then someone spotted me and called me over. It was a gentleman named Gene Martin. He was an amazing singer and dancer who often opened A.A. Allen's meetings for him. Gene needed a job doing – there were a pile of flyers that needed stamping. He put me to work. Talk about boring. It took me hours, but I dutifully completed the task.

Then, just as I was finishing up, A.A. Allen himself appeared to give me my "wages" for this task. Unbelievably he handed over a One Pound note, a Ten Shilling note and two half-crowns. I had never seen so much money before. It was almost embarrassing. Together my two half-crowns had been worth a total of five shillings. Now I had thirty-five shillings. God had returned my offering seven times over.

That day I learned a lesson I would never forget – one that would stand me in good stead for the rest of my life. Whatever is given to God comes back, with much more besides.

Someone once asked me, "When did you find out you had a propensity for being successful? Were you taught it? Did you learn how to do it? Did it just come upon you?" All I know is, what happened, happened. But I do believe that God rewards those whose bank accounts He is allowed to raid from time to time.

My experience is that what God uses, He replaces quickly and in far greater measure. I am an entrepreneur and a quick learner, so as soon as I realised I could trust God to meet my needs and more, I made sure He realised He could use my cheque book whenever He wanted.

He's never once left me out of pocket.

GIVING IN FAITH

Sedley's example rubbed off on me. He imparted a profoundly important life lesson: those whom God can trust with a little can be trusted with a lot.

Those who are good stewards and can give out their resources – even when to do so might cost them personally – are ideal candidates to be given more. This principle is amply illustrated throughout the Bible.

Just before Julie and I married, we had our eye on buying a house in Mulbarton, south of Norwich. We were intending to buy it off-plan. There was a corner plot available that would be completed just in time for us to move in when we arrived home from our honeymoon. One day Sedley mentioned, in passing, that he was selling a property he owned on Patterson Road. Then he said that when the sale was completed we could have the money! It was almost a throw away comment. We couldn't believe it. It was so unexpected and, as a wedding present, generous beyond anything we could have imagined.

But it was all the more amazing considering something that had happened a few days earlier. Julie and I were at church and there was a special offering being taken for a minister called David Greenow. Everyone was encouraged to give as much as they could. Over the preceding months, week by week, we had saved a few pounds – every penny we could muster, in fact – as we prepared for our future. But we both felt God speak to us about giving sacrificially. We were to give away all we had saved and honour Him in doing so. As the offering basket came round the congregation Julie and I looked at each other and we both knew. The full amount of our savings went into the offering, just as my two half-crowns had done years before.

We told no one about it. Sedley didn't know. All we knew was that it was right and we'd done it. We'd emptied our account as we felt right before God. The amount we subsequently received back as a wedding gift was probably twenty times what we had given away. We discovered that God is no man's debtor. He loves to reward unconditional giving on the part of His children.

GOD'S FAVOUR

There is a common saying, "You reap what you sow." It is often couched in the negative, as a kind of threat. In fact, it is a principle that is threaded throughout the whole of Scripture. Although it can have negative connotations, mostly in the Bible it is expressed positively: if we sow well, we will reap a reward.

God rewards those who live with a generous spirit. Just as in the examples above, if we "sow" our money into God's work, He will ensure we are blessed as a result. Some have taken this thought to extremes, which has resulted in the excesses of TV evangelists who only ever seem to talk about money. That is not what I'm referring to. We don't give in order to get. We give unconditionally. It is up to God how He sees fit to bless us as a result. As with my two half-crowns, sometimes there will be a generous influx of funds to replace what we've given. At other times, we may just know God's favour. Doors open for us that would normally remain shut. The following is a story about just that.

UNMERITED FAVOUR

After helping to run our family car business for a number of years, the time came when it made sense for me to take it over and run it as my own concern. This was great, in theory, because I had proven that I could run it successfully. My problem was that I had no capital behind me. I would need a rather large loan from the bank in order to buy the business and its assets from my parents. I rang the local manager at Barclays Bank and asked for an appointment.

The banking hall at Bank Plain was 150 feet long and 50 feet high. It was a huge, cavernous building. That day it was as intimidating to me as it was beautiful to look at. I had zero experience dealing with bank managers and I was nervous. Entering the bank, I had to walk the entire length of the hall. Like a scene from a Harry Potter movie, the eyes of the cashiers bored into me as my footsteps echoed loudly. To say I felt self-conscious was an understatement. I felt like I had come to rob the bank, when all I wanted was a loan!

After I had become a Christian I began reading the Bible regularly. Some verses that always stuck in my memory were from the book of Proverbs:

> *"My son, forget not my law; let your heart keep my commandments ... So shall you find favour in the sight of God and man."* (Proverbs 3:1-4)

If ever I needed favour it was today. The bank manager wasn't God, but it seemed to me that he was in control of my more immediate circumstances. I needed to borrow £200,000 in order to fund the business buyout. To put that into perspective, I had never earned more than £3,500 per annum up until that point, which was a pretty respectable amount. £200,000 was therefore an audacious, astronomical amount for a young man like me to be asking for.

I navigated past the last of the cashiers and was confronted by the smart commissionaire who stood before me like a guard in front of the double doors that led into the manager's suite. I explained I had an appointment. He looked at me disdainfully and pointed to where I should sit and wait. Didn't utter a word. To add to my humiliation there were people working in the balcony above me, looking down to see if I was anyone important. Clearly not. If I had any confidence to begin with, by now it had drained out of me. It seemed like an eternity until the commissionaire signalled for me to follow him.

I entered the manager's office. He was seated in a big leather chair behind an equally large, elegant oak desk. He lifted his eyes towards me in a "what can I do for you?" kind of way. I wish that somebody had told me back then that the best way to make a presentation is to memorise how you will start and how you will end. If you can at least nail the beginning and the end, more often than not the rest will fall into place. Later I learned the art of borrowing money. But today, I had no idea.

I falteringly explained that my parents had decided to retire and that I was hoping – in fact, needing – to buy them out. Plus I actually needed £200,000 to do that. I can't remember much else. I recall he asked me what experience I had in running the business. I told him I had been involved since day one and had been responsible for buying and selling most of the cars. I couldn't have told him much more than that, because I didn't know much more than that!

He looked me up and down. I could see by his face that he was pondering my request. I was possibly his first appointment of the afternoon. In those days, the managers and directors of a bank had their own dedicated kitchen on the premises and a fully stocked wine cellar to boot. As a result, they were invariably more accommodating after lunch than before it I later discovered.

At the end of our discussion he reached for a small box on his desk, lifted the lid and extracted a new business card. "What did you say your name was?" he asked. I told him and he scribbled it on the card in pencil. Then he turned it over and wrote, in longhand, "Overdraft agreed for two hundred thousand pounds for one year. Repayable on demand." He stood, signifying the end of our meeting and looked at me. "I really hope everything works as planned," he said. "Do let me know how you are getting on."

And that was that.

I exited back through the double doors and retraced my steps through the echoing hall. This time my back was straight and my head held high. It appeared to me as though the cashiers were sheepishly avoiding my stare behind their glass screens – proven wrong on this occasion! I had indeed found favour and in less than an hour I had been given all I needed to go into business on my own. It was a life-changing day, though I had no idea where it would all lead. Ephesians 3:20 talks about the God who can do, "exceedingly abundantly more than we can ask or imagine." He would prove that to me again and again in the years that followed.

THE SECRET OF GIVING

As well as teaching that those who give to God will be blessed, the Bible highlights a specific method of giving and gives clear instructions on how to go about it. It also speaks about what the results of following this practice will be. "Tithing" is the practice of giving a fixed percentage of your income back to God (through the local church or to specific ministries or trusts, for example) and goes right back to the beginning of biblical history. It involves giving away 10% of your annual income. Some people query this practice. 10% sounds like a lot to them. But we get to keep 90%; at least it's not the other way around! At least it's not like VAT either, which was first levied on our used car profits in 1971 at a rate of 7.5% and has never gone below that since. Today one sixth of your margin is needed to help balance the books. Tithing has been fixed at 10% from the beginning.

Since God is not short of a bob or two, why does He need us to tithe, you might wonder? It is to demonstrate our honour and obedience towards Him. It acknowledges the fact that all we have comes from Him. It also gives us an opportunity to show ourselves faithful in the good stewardship of His resources. It demonstrates that we can control our finances, rather than them controlling us.

Both Julie and I have practised the principle of tithing since before we were married. Here is the deal: we have faithfully given 10% of everything we have ever made back to God. We have done so joyfully and willingly, rather than religiously and grudgingly. We have left the results of this in God's hands. He doesn't like us to try and negotiate what we will get back. But over the years we have found that either our 90% has miraculously "stretched" to become more effective than the 100%, or out of the blue, according to His favour, some unexpected blessing has come our way.

You may look at this and say, "That's ridiculous, you've just been lucky." But I remember a comment someone once made: "Isn't it remarkable – the harder I work the luckier I become." I have worked hard and I have continued to give 10% to God, even during the times when it was hard to do so. As a result I believe He has blessed my endeavours.

The verses I quoted from the book of Proverbs continue, with further advice that can help us to position ourselves for God's blessing:

"My son, do not forget my law.
Let your heart keep my commandments.
If you do you will find favour and high esteem in the sight of God and man.
Trust in the Lord with all your heart.
Lean not on your own understanding.
In all your ways acknowledge Him and He shall direct your paths.
Do not be clever in you own eyes.
Regard the Lord and stay away from evil.
It will be health to your body and strength to your bones.
Honour the Lord with your possessions and with the firstfruits of your increase.
If you do that your barns will be filled with plenty and your vats will overflow with new wine."
(Proverbs 3:1-10)

Without doubt this has been one of the secrets of our success. We have tithed 10% of everything, morning, noon and night. As a result our net worth increased every year, sometimes embarrassingly so. From time to time we have increased our giving, just to see what God will do. Each time He trumps us. We cannot out-give Him.

One of the downsides of being successful is that there is a constant stream of people who feel that you could and should be supporting them/their cause. Since 2006 we have received around three requests per postal delivery requesting funds. At one time we tried to respond personally to each request, but it proved a full time job to keep on top of. Now we just set aside a sum of money at the start of each year that is targeted for local giving. That way we don't upset people.

There are many causes we could support, but mostly we have chosen to invest in the lives of the young people in our own area, which we do through the Lind Trust. Over the years we have not personally needed all that we have earned, so much of these funds have gone into the Trust. The trustees are responsible for using and distributing its income. One of the better known projects in Norwich to receive our support was the Open Youth Venue. It required an investment of something over £10 million, but has provided a unique resource for the young people of Norwich. You can discover more about it online. More recently the trustees have acquired the former Fire Station in Bethel Street, Norwich. Investment will be required to repurpose this venue and put it to good community use.

I came to Norfolk in 1970 with practically nothing. The only asset I owned was my motorbike. In Norfolk I found faith in God. Since then He has enabled me to be successful and to give away more than I ever dreamt of earning. I give Him all the credit for this. It is both humbling and amazing.

But I think the most generous are those who are prepared to give of themselves – their time, their hearts, their gratitude, their appreciation. This is true generosity of spirit. God gave of Himself in order to reach out to broken humanity. I still find the love of God incomprehensible. He sacrificed His Son in order to save us. How can we possibly respond to this? Could a valid response be that we seek to be similarly lavish in our giving? The Bible says that,

> *"He who refreshes [others], will himself be refreshed"* (Proverbs 11:25).

May we all live for the good of others and know the joy of generosity.

LEAVING A LEGACY

I cannot say that I have ever heard God speak to me audibly. But I will, however, never be able to forget the day that His inaudible voice told me – as clearly as if He had been speaking out loud – that one day I would be responsible for building for Him a church for all ages, from the cradle to the grave. This word from God stayed with me and I wondered how, at some time in the future, it would materialise.

It began with a conversation with my friend Bob Gordon as we chatted over supper one Sunday night. We were discussing the need for a new building for the church – a permanent home; a place that would be more than just a building, but also a resource centre and a hub for all kinds of activities.

It was always dangerous to mention money around Bob. Being the visionary leader that he was, both his faith and his imagination immediately ran away with him. Earlier that day I'd made an offhand comment, saying that we probably needed around 10 million dollars to service our needs. It was an absurd comment, considering our purely Sterling environment. But Bob was quite happy. He could do a lot with the £7.7 million pounds it translated into. The trouble was, I was merely repeating out loud what I felt I'd heard God say to me. What the man of God heard was me committing myself to somehow raising £7.7m to give him, to build the church. Either way, we now knew two things: one day we would build a church and we would need £7.7m to do it.

Fast forward to 2006…

Julie and I were chatting in the snug next to our kitchen. We were two or three weeks away from the point of no return in selling our business.

"Are you sure we should sell it?" I asked her.

"You know we are," she replied. "You said it was getting too much. You needed a buyer. I prayed for one and one came along. Of course I'm sure!"

Then she asked me exactly how much we were making from the sale. I said it was a lot. How much is a lot, came the response. I told her it was more than we'd ever need, being slightly evasive. But she said, how much is that, not being a person who is easily fobbed off. I did the calculations on a small pocket calculator.

- £x for good will
- £x for liquidating the net assets
- £x uplift on company portfolio
- £x on the sale of properties we owned personally
- £x to account for smaller liabilities we were walking away from

After carefully considering all the factors I hit the total button. I will never forget what it all amounted to: £77,777,768. I must have lost £9 in the rounding up, otherwise it was a round £77,777,777. God's bit – my tithe – would be £7.7m. It was the exact amount that God foretold should be set aside to build a church.

At that moment I heard God's voice speak to me: "When you started, you set out to make £7.7m in order to build a church. You would have given it all away to do so." (And I would have). "Because it was in your heart to do this, you can keep the rest."

My accountant, John Savery, who is not a man of faith, does my tax return each year. That year the gross charitable donation that appeared on my return was £7,777,777. These were the funds earmarked to build a church in Norwich that would one day become Today's Lifestyle Church (TLC). I may have ended up with the task of the acquisition and development of the site, but God was paying for it with funds that resulted from His incredible favour. It was simply unbelievable.

God can produce so much from so little. He can do the most with the least. Everything with nothing. Mine is a "much more" God!

Making or earning a great amount of money is a burden that should not, and cannot, be taken lightly. Many may find this a strange comment to make and prefer to agree with Spike Milligan who once said, "All I ask is the chance to prove that money can't make me happy!" But having a large amount of money at your disposal can create more problems than it solves.

Whenever I hear about someone inheriting or winning a fortune, I usually feel sorry for them. Especially Lottery winners; mega-winners all the more. What appears to be incredible can often turn to distress. Having too much can be a nightmare. Why? Because assets quickly turn into liabilities. The more you have, the more time you spend worrying about them and trying to manage them. The number of advisors you need to hire is seemingly endless. You begin by assuming that you can manage everything yourself, but you quickly realise that you can't. And if you don't manage your money well, someone else will invariably end up doing it for you.

The second, and perhaps greater, danger is that often the recipient doesn't have the character to handle such a sudden influx of wealth. Suddenly having access to vast amounts of money can ruin a person if they don't have the good character and grounding to sustain themselves. Few do. A long line of rock stars who have lived to excess is testament to the fact and but one example.

I believe God prepared me for what was to come later. He sought to shape my character earlier on and helped me to become faithful in small, relatively insignificant things. Gradually, over time, He was able to trust me with more.

I often reflect on the parable recounted in Matthew chapter 25. Jesus told a story about a man whose master gave him five talents (the currency of the day). He traded with them and ended up making his master five more. Another servant was given two talents and he also managed to double them to four. Then there was the man who was given just one talent. He seemed to be both risk and work averse. Instead of putting the money to work by trading or investing it, he simply buried it in the ground in order to keep it "safe".

Later the master called his three servants together and asked them to report back. While two had made significant increases, the third servant had to hand back the single talent he'd kept, saying, "Here, have what is yours." The master responded angrily, telling him off and then giving the one talent to the man who had already made ten. Jesus offered the following unusual explanation for this:

> *"For to everyone who has, more will be given, and he will have abundance; but from him who does not have, even what he has will be taken away."* (Matthew 25:29)

Why should I have been given so much? Was it because I could handle it? I've tried to use my resources to honour God, though I've not always succeeded. Was it because I'm talented? I'm not sure that I am. Was it because I needed it? With hindsight I probably didn't! I believe it comes down to simple, faithful stewardship and continued giving.

In terms of character, I think my saving grace has been a secure relationship with God and the ability to look beyond this life – to see the bigger picture. At best we only lease the things we think we "own", because we leave this life with nothing.

For a few weeks after we made the sale of our company we amused ourselves by thinking we could do anything we wanted; go anywhere. But that soon wore off as we reflected on just how happy we'd been over the years at Ash Tree Farm. Some may look at us and think we didn't maximise our opportunity. All I can say is that over the years I have not found the super-wealthy to be correspondingly happy or peaceful. We have continued to live as we've always done – and it's unlikely we'll ever change.

My advice to you is: *cultivate a spirit of generosity and in sowing, you will be amazed at what you reap.*

EPILOGUE: THE PRODIGAL SON

"While he was still a long way off, his father saw him coming."

– LUKE 15:11-32

I didn't go into a sauna looking for God. If I'd been looking for Him, I'd have gone to a church.

In truth, I wasn't absolutely sure He existed at all. And I was less than sure that knowing God would be anything other than a handicap. God, of course, had other plans. I was expecting a sauna. What I got was something greater than anything I could have anticipated.

It was in the early 1970s that Pastor Sedley Pimlott began buying cars from us. I noticed right away that he was a fascinating character and struck me as being a little eccentric. I never thought that he would eventually become my father-in-law. Sedley would buy lovely cars for other people – a Jaguar and a Vauxhall Cresta for his sons – whilst he drove around in something far more utilitarian. In fact, Sedley bought cars for everyone: his daughters, his brother. Then he also bought and gave away cars to people outside of his family. I never could understand why.

Sedley made it clear to me that he was a Christian, a church Pastor, and he often invited me to come and visit his church. I wasn't up for being preached at, so I made every effort to stay out of harm's way. I made one excuse or another; politely declining. I never once went along. Then one day he invited me round to his house. Underlining his flair and ingenuity, Sedley had built a sauna in an old railway carriage in his back garden. He spent many a happy hour there socialising. On this particular day he had invited me to come and chat to him whilst having a sauna.

Sedley made himself comfortable on the lower bench, while I was more confident sitting up higher. I didn't realise it was hotter up top, but I survived. As usual we talked about cars, business and our families. Then he said to me, "Before you go, Graham, I'd like to share something with you." He began to recount in detail Jesus' parable about the Prodigal Son.

At no point had I sought to have an "encounter" with God. If anything, I was intent on not having a relationship with Him. But as Sedley spoke, the Holy Spirit was at work in my heart. I knew it too. I felt something happening. In faith I responded as best I could to what I sensed was God reaching out to me. It felt like I was taking a huge risk – jumping off the proverbial cliff edge, not knowing whether God really existed or not. But I was suddenly willing to take the chance, just in case He did.

Allow me to paraphrase the parable in my own words and share the effect it had on me:

A man had two sons. His firstborn was a steady-eddy, the younger more colourful. The older was happy to stay at home and serve, but the younger son wanted to live life to the full. One day he said to his father, "Give me the portion of inheritance that falls to me. I don't want it when you die – I want it now." The father divided up his assets and gave the son what was due to him. He gave him his requested inheritance. Without a second thought, the son packed a bag and hurriedly departed for a far off country.

While the inheritance lasted the younger son enjoyed it to the full, indulging in everything and everyone on offer. But when his money ran out, so did his friends. His fortunes spiralled downward until he ended up doing the lowest kind of manual labour available in his society – feeding pigs. He was so hungry he was forced to consider eating some of the pig food himself, just to stay alive.

Eventually, he realised that his wild lifestyle had cost him more than just his inheritance. He had all but destroyed his relationship with his father. Then he had an epiphany. The Bible says, "He came to himself."

> *"My father's servants have bread enough and I perish with hunger. I will go back to my father and say, 'I am not worthy to be called your son. Make me as one of your hired servants.'"*

He got up, left the pig sty, set off on the long trek back to his father's house.

On the flip side of this story was a man who so loved his son that he allowed him to make his own choices and didn't try to control him. He allowed him to live life his way. But he never stopped loving him.

Each night after dinner the father went up onto his rooftop and looked out for his son. Day after day, night after night, he looked to the horizon, but each time he was disappointed. Then, one day, he saw a familiar shape, way off up the dusty road. It was a frame he instantly recognised; the one he had so longed to see.

He didn't think twice. He just ran. Out of the house, down the road, until he reached his dirty, dishevelled boy. He fell on him and kissed him, hugged him, welcomed him home.

The son launched into his well-rehearsed repentance speech: "Father, I've sinned against heaven and against you. I am no longer worthy to be called your son. If I could just…"

But his father would have none of it; he cut off his speech. This was the best day of his life. His prayers had been answered. The one he loved had returned. His boy, his flesh and blood, had come home.

By then the servants had caught up with the father and he issued some instructions: "Fetch me the best robe; find me a ring; bring some kid leather for his feet … kill the fatted calf, because my son who was dead, is alive! He was lost, but is now found. Let's go and celebrate. It's time to party!"

For me the story needed little explanation. At that moment I was very aware that I, too, had taken my life into my own hands. My parents had a personal relationship with God, but I did not. It hadn't been for me. I had chosen not to follow in their footsteps and I was living far away from Him. I had messed up.

What touched my heart was the great love of the father. Each day he had looked for his son, longing for him to return home. When he finally saw him, he dropped everything and ran to embrace him. There were no words of recrimination. The father wasn't looking for an apology. He was looking to restore a relationship. There was a total lack of condemnation. A great compassion instead. An overwhelming love.

The best robe was fetched. The family ring for his hand. The kid leather for his bloodied feet. There was immediate repatriation. Instant restoration. Unconditional acceptance. The father's big heart; his great joy; his joyful testimony…

Emotion flooded my being as I sensed God's love for me. The hugeness of His heart; His desire for relationship with me; His love for me, personally. Suddenly, God moved from being the Creator of the Universe, distant, unknowable, impersonal, to being a Father – my Father. It wasn't about God and His relationship to the universe. It wasn't about God and His relationship to mankind. It was just about Him and me.

My memory of what followed remains something of a blur. I knelt down and tried to pray. I remember Sedley praying. Suddenly realising that the God I didn't know existed, until a moment ago, was everywhere. I remember saying sorry to Him. Tears flowed. I remember being naked. I remember saying, "Amen." I sensed God reaching out to me. I felt as though we were alone, just Him and me. No criticism, no condemnation. Nothing but love and compassion. I was overwhelmed by His gentleness, graciousness and love. I didn't resist. I couldn't have if I'd tried.

The most amazing thing was, from that instant, there was no way back. I was now in relationship with God and He with me. I often say I came out of that sauna very pink on the outside, but white as snow on the inside. I was aware that my sin had gone. All the wrong things I'd done in the past, erased. I felt clean. Something had changed in my heart.

I felt a sense of peace. I had a spring in my step and a huge smile on my face. It's not easy to explain, but I felt like I finally had hope. As though life – real life – could now begin. I couldn't wait [illegible]o start the adventure. I had no idea what lay ahead, but it really [illegible]dn't matter. My future lay in God's hands and, unequivocally, I [illegible] it would be good.

[illegible] day I returned home wide eyed, my head spinning. I passed [illegible] drive home to Long Stratton knowing that something [illegible]arily significant had just taken place. I felt free, light, excited. Then I had questions: Would it last? Was my experience of God's presence really real or had I imagined it? What was I going to tell my Mum? Had I just become religious? Would I go to church? Would I enjoy it?

But the questions didn't matter that evening. Something had happened. I felt clean, alive and excited. I wasn't sure what I had to be excited about, but it didn't matter! As I lay in bed, I reflected on an amazing night. I knew that I was saved.

I slept very well. The instant I awoke the next morning, I knew. I knew I was different. Something had changed in me. I felt new and fresh. I told Mum and Dad all about it the moment I saw them. Later I told everyone in the garage workshop who would listen. Some did listen. Others laughed, thinking I'd lost it. I wasn't concerned. I was delighted to acknowledge my new found relationship with Jesus.

With hindsight, I can say that the past 40 years have been amazing. Finding faith in God was the best thing that ever happened to me. Nothing has mesmerised me, contained me, fulfilled me or satisfied me like knowing God. For me, my faith in God defines me as a person. Without Him I would have been an unhappy, empty shell. Today I can live for something beyond myself because He has given me an eternal perspective.

If you have never experienced it for yourself, the same great love and compassion of God is there for you. He longs to be in relationship with you and to show you that your life can
all it was intended to be – and much, much more – if
surrender to Him; allow Him to pour His life into

Take a risk. Jump off the cliff. You surely
and everything to gain. I know you wil